Praise for *Jos*

"*Josiah's Fire* is a must-read. You will be encouraged, compelled, and deeply moved to see God's love and power in and through little Josiah. As you ponder this young autistic boy's amazing visitations and revelations, heavenly dimensions and mysteries of the kingdom of God will be revealed to you."

– PATRICIA KING, author, television host, and founder of Patricia King Ministries, www.patriciaking.com

"In the mystery and majesty of God, He divinely places His glory in clay pots. Indeed, His grace is sufficient and even magnified in our weaknesses. Occasionally, it seems the Lord takes extra efforts to display His wonders. Such is the case in the life of young Josiah. This precious pure vessel is a steward of a mighty gift from the Holy Spirit. Get ready because the authentic testimonies in this mind-blowing book will leave you shocked, stunned, and hungry for more of God."

– DR. JAMES W. GOLL, founder of God Encounters, Life Language trainer, and international best-selling author

"Families are struggling. This out-of-this-world book offers fresh hope."

– DR. KEVIN LEMAN, *New York Times* best-selling author of *The Birth Order Book*

"Have you ever wondered if God, heaven, and angels are actually real? If so, you will enjoy *Josiah's Fire*, a fascinating true story of a little boy caught in the grip of autism. Everything comes crashing down on the Cullen family—until Josiah learns to communicate. Although Josiah is limited in his physical body by autism, his writings impact the world. Get ready to encounter a sign and a wonder as you learn God's ways through the eyes and ears of this young messenger!"

– BRIAN AND CANDICE SIMMONS, *The Passion Translation* project

"Don't miss this profound book! *Josiah's Fire* is a captivating true account of a family that encountered faith, hope, and a vision of the heavenlies through an extraordinary journey with their autistic son. This book is not only for families of children with disabilities—it's a dramatic, spellbinding story that will increase your desire to draw closer to God and hear his voice, and it will deepen your longing for heaven."

> – CAROL KENT, internationally acclaimed speaker and award-winning author of *When I Lay My Isaac Down*

"*Josiah's Fire* is one of those books you can't put down. A family faces a profound challenge, but a small child leads the way in a beautiful, hope-filled journey to a new way of living and looking at faith, love, and the way the universe just might really work (if we could only see the world as Josiah does). Josiah is an unlikely poet and prophet, and I'm certain you'll fall in love with him as I did."

> – SUSY FLORY, *New York Times* author or coauthor of eleven books, including the runaway bestseller, *Thunder Dog*

"*Josiah's Fire* opened a whole new world of thinking to me, making me ponder how God moves and communicates to those who have ears to hear. I found myself rapt with attention as I moved from page to page, often on the verge of tears, often on the verge of laughing out loud. Why 'on the verge'? Because what I read awed me to the degree that it was near impossible to cry or laugh. This excellently written book will give hope to many. Truly a story that had to be told."

> – MIKE SHREVE, pastor, evangelist, and bestselling author of *65 Promises from God for Your Child* and *In Search of the True Light*

"*Josiah's Fire* is the breath of heaven released through one boy on earth. Josiah's amazing supernatural journey is filled with life-altering God-encounters and angelic visitations. The Father chose Josiah as an emissary to share revelation directly from the throne. He shares many truths about heaven and the nature of the triune God. Through Josiah's parents' struggle with their son's autistic personality, God reveals his love and concern for all people, no matter what handicaps or difficulties they face. Full of hope and love, these pages will empower you to live from victory to victory."

– JOAN HUNTER, author and evangelist,
www.joanhunter.org

"*Josiah's Fire* is informative, compelling, and poignant, immediately drawing readers into a wild, fascinating ride with the Cullen family. Biblical truth meets heartfelt joy when little Josiah sees and hears in a realm that's unavailable to most of us. This is one of the most inspiring true stories I have come across in a very long time."

– KATHI MACIAS, speaker and award-winning author
of more than fifty books, www.kathimacias.com

"What this young autistic boy teaches us about heaven and earth is mind-boggling and fascinating as it lifts the veil between two worlds. Tahni Cullen will never get over the diagnosis that changed her family forever, but through the devastation, a miracle is born. Josiah gives his mom, and all the rest of us, a glimpse into that place where pain-filled people can laugh again. Cheryl Ricker, a masterful storyteller of true stories, coauthors this intriguing tale of supernatural touches and crazy love. Brace yourself: *Josiah's Fire* will grip you with holy flames from the first few words."

– ANITA AGERS BROOKS, CPT, CCS, CLTF,
common trauma expert, international speaker, and award-
winning author of *Getting through What You Can't Get Over*

"Wow. *Josiah's Fire.* Total wonderment. It is otherworldly, utterly remarkable, nearly unbelievable. And yet, I humbly and reverently believe in a God who can do anything, with anyone, at any time, and in any way he sees fit. Few are graced with gifts as special as have been given to this precious boy. I can't help but stand in awe of the Good Gift-Giver himself. To God be the glory. Great things he is doing through this amazing family's must-read story."

– CHERI KEAGGY, Dove Award-winning recording artist, songwriter, speaker, blogger, www.cherikeaggy.com

"I've learned that the ones who society considers *least*, God often uses *most*. And adversity often puts us on God's varsity. Josiah is no exception. This remarkable lad has autism, but autism doesn't have him! There's no limit to what God can do with a totally surrendered life. This powerful book will stretch and propel you on your journey with Jesus. Buy one for yourself and ten to give away! Your friends will thank you for it."

– FRANK SHELTON, author, Fox News contributor, Washington, DC field representative for *My Hope with Billy Graham* and the *Franklin Graham Decision America Tour*

"Scripture states we must become like little children to enter the kingdom of heaven. *Josiah's Fire* is a story of redemption, hope, and God's big love speaking through a speechless little boy with autism. Young Josiah has a spiritual depth unmatched by many adults, and a knowledge of heaven not found in books. It's also a story of a mother's love, persistence, and sacrifice to help the world hear words her son cannot vocalize. Brilliant writing turns this true story into a page-turning, awe-inspiring glimpse into a gifted mind and a miracle-performing God. You'll want to read this book even if you don't know about autism but want to know more about heaven."

– JANET THOMPSON, founder of Woman to Woman Mentoring, speaker, freelance editor, and author of eighteen books, including *Forsaken God? Remembering the Goodness of God Our Culture Has Forgotten*

"*Josiah's Fire* is an *amazing* experience! Through a surprising and unusual communication method, a young boy struggling with severe autism opens a world of stunning intelligence, mysterious insights—and heaven. The descriptions of angelic activity are extremely convincing. But more than that, you'll view God through new eyes. Josiah will hold you spellbound with his beyond-captivating experiences in heaven that are both revelatory and revolutionary. Very few books have held me captive, making me sacrifice sleep and time—but this book did! Read it and you'll find yourself more empowered to joyfully participate with heaven on earth."

– MARK HENDRICKSON, Dwelling Place Ministries,
author of *Supernatural Provision*

"Touching! Riveting! Inspirational … hard to put it down. I highly recommend *Josiah's Fire!*"

– DR. JEFFREY SEIF, Distinguished Professor of Biblical
and Jewish Studies, Kings University

"I am a journalist and a skeptic and can spot a fake a mile away. Believe me, Josiah Cullen is no fake. Without knowing a thing about me, Josiah wrote twenty-three details of my life that *no one* could have possibly known except through the Spirit of God. This ten-year-old, non-verbal autistic boy gave me messages that changed my life, always bringing me back to Jesus and the Word of God. *Josiah's Fire* is life changing from start to finish and had me in tears before I finished."

– MAX DAVIS, author of more than thirty books, including
*Dead Dog Like Me* and *When Jesus Was a Green-Eyed Brunette*

"As Josiah's former ABA therapist, I had the pleasure of witnessing his hard work and courage. After Josiah's communication breakthrough, Tahni and I discussed the validity of his statements, and Josiah and I typed letters back and forth about his challenges, desires, and fears. Josiah is a great example of how a soul lies beyond the physical, and why it is so vital to treat all children with equity and worth. These children have abilities that can revolutionize people who are open to receive their gifted messages. Josiah's voice opens doors to spiritual understanding, and I am excited for him to share it with the world. "

– KIMBERLY ZESZUTEK, MA, NCC, LPC,
intern, Filtering Light Counseling in Portland, Oregon

"I couldn't put it down. *Josiah's Fire* is a story of hope and joy in the midst of pain. The entertaining and refreshing stories make you look at life through new lenses. Josiah's insights are amazing. His life reminds us that it's a blessing to look at light over darkness and that we don't need to let our pain and disabilities hinder us from our God-given destinies."

– DR. GERSHOM SIKAALA, author of *You Shall Live* and
*A New Dimension of Glory,* www.gershomsikaala.org

"I am privileged to know Tahni Cullen personally. She is a woman of the Word and prayer, who loves God deeply and lives what she believes. A few weeks after I first met Tahni, her nine-year-old son, Josiah, gave me a powerful message that spoke profoundly and personally about my ministry and the people-group I work with thousands of miles away. Josiah's words were so unbelievably accurate that they reduced me to tears and awe-struck worship of God. Each chapter of *Josiah's Fire* helps us better understand a personal, ever-present God who longs to communicate with us, redeem our pain, and draw us closer to his heart."

– REV. RUTH TUTTLE CONARD,
author of *Designer Women: Made by God*

"It is impossible that any young child, let alone a child with autism, could ever contain this level of remarkable insight. Truly, Josiah has been given a gift directly from the Lord. A gift that will grow, transform, and teach others to see and understand God's treasures in the deep places. I highly recommend this beautiful, transparent, page-turner story of a grappling family that finds radical hope in the most surprising way."

– PAUL RAPLEY, international healing evangelist,
www.paulrapley.com

"I have known the Cullen family for fifteen years, and Tahni is a trusted friend and ministry partner, who I have watched respond in obedience to God in the most trying circumstances. I know how incredibly difficult it was for her to face the risks of sharing this story. Tahni cared more about God's thoughts toward her than anything else. Each chapter, rich in the reality of God's love and presence, is a reassurance that our 'yes' to God is always worth it."

– SUSAN LENNARTSON, minister, author, speaker, coach,
grandmother in touch with autism

"This compelling, beautifully written true story unveils what can happen when an ordinary family is thrust into extraordinary circumstances. Not only does *Josiah's Fire* sing with uniqueness, style, and all the right story elements of a notable page-turner, but it grabs your heart from start to finish and won't let go."

– DENISE GEORGE, author of thirty books,
nonfiction writing teacher, www.bookwritingbootcamp.org

"Amazing, inspiring, true story about my new favorite little boy, Josiah. This book shouts from the mountaintops that *nothing is impossible with God*! When you buy this book, be sure to get a second copy for someone who struggles to trust him. Step by step, you'll be blown away by the honest fact that God not only has a detailed plan for you and your family members—but also that he loves to fulfill his plan for those with less than perfect faith. Read this book, and you will proclaim as I did, 'Is there anything too difficult for our God?' "

– STEVE SHULTZ, founder of *The Elijah List*

# Josiah's Fire

## Autism stole his words, God gave him a voice

# TAHNI CULLEN
### with Cheryl Ricker

**BroadStreet**
PUBLISHING

BroadStreet Publishing Group, LLC
Racine, Wisconsin, USA
BroadStreetPublishing.com

Josiah's Fire: Autism Stole His Words, God Gave Him a Voice

Stock or custom editions of BroadStreet Publishing titles may be purchased in bulk for educational, business, ministry, fundraising, or sales promotional use. For information, please e-mail info@broadstreetpublishing.com.

Cover by Garborg Design at GarborgDesign.com
Interior by Katherine Lloyd at theDESKonline.com

Printed in the United States of America

16 17 18 19 20 5 4 3 2

# AUTHORS' NOTE

When little Josiah had his communication miracle on the iPad in 2012, he typed a single stream of words without spaces or punctuation, all saved verbatim. For readability, we have added spaces and punctuation and corrected occasional misspellings. For brevity, we have omitted words and sentences.

# CONTENTS

## Prologue

# Josiah's Fire

*No known cause. No known cure. Lifelong.*

The diagnosis hammered in my head like a prison sentence as we sped home in our Corolla. The forty-minute trek against the howling wind felt like a trip to the cemetery to bury our dreams.

I'd grieved deep when Dad died, but I'd been able to move on. Not so with this kind of progressive death, which threatened to crush me with its ongoing torment.

I glanced back at Josiah whose sky-blue eyes, once full of life, now stared blankly into space. Where did he go? To that same faraway place that held his words hostage? Prized words like *Mama, Daddy, cookie,* and *bumblebee.* Would I even remember their sounds from his lips?

Joe and I absorbed thick silence while the unseen beast of autism pressed with its loud taunt. "I'll make your life crazy difficult," it hissed. "No matter where you go, I'll be right there in the backseat following you."

# 1

# I'm Losing Him

"If I could talk, I would never get bad news."
– Josiah Cullen

**August 18, 2007**

When a nuclear bomb explodes, no one can predict the extent of its devastation. I'll never forget the day when I discovered this also applies to an emotional bomb.

As Joe and I hunkered around the dining table with his parents, the clock ticked, the barbeque sauce dripped off our plates in the sink, and I smiled at the thought of our twenty-two-month-old, lost in his dream world down the hall.

Joe's parents had returned for their second visit in two weeks, this time to take their car to the Twin Cities, because apparently, we had a better selection of British car parts than the shops in North Dakota.

Frank leaned in, talking in his usual casual New York accent. "This isn't an easy topic, but we need to share something with you."

I straightened. "Okay …"

"We don't want to alarm you," he said.

Too late. My mind had already shot into danger mode. Was it Frank or Kathy? Was one of them sick? What could be wrong?

A few hours earlier, Pastor Bob had preached about storms. "You're either going into one, you're in one, or you're coming out."

His message reminded me of Joe, who had a stroke four years ago. It also reminded me of Dad, who had a fatal heart attack four years before that. These past four years, though, had been nothing but smooth sailing. God had given us a charming house in a quaint neighborhood. He'd even thrown in a home daycare down the street and a nearby playmate for our son.

Josiah. What a gift. That morning as we sat in Kohl's parking lot, I'd laughed aloud as he and Joe played eye games in the rearview mirror. I loved their bond, and I could hardly wait to see how it would grow through the years.

The room quieted as Frank cleared his throat. "Josiah doesn't seem as interested in us as he used to be. Uh, how do I say this? Toddlers are usually more interactive."

I stiffened. "What do you mean?"

"Well, we don't want to alarm you, but we heard a radio interview on NPR, and they talked about autism."

"Autism?" Thick clouds rolled into my thoughts as the word twisted my gut. What was he suggesting … that something was wrong with our son?

"We're not saying we know what's going on. We have no idea. But we noticed a few things that got us thinking."

Joe stayed calm. "What kind of things?"

"Well, last weekend he wasn't as interested in his cousin Keenan as usual. Then, when Kathy and I returned home, we talked about how he acted when he came to our house three months ago. He kept looking at the patterns in the chain link fence. Kinda all business about it."

The clouds darkened, gathering force. Unwelcomed images flashed across my mind. The cousin, the fence, the staring. I'd read articles about autism, and I'd always breathed a sigh of relief, saying, *Thank God that isn't my child.*

Kathy shrugged. "We just think it would be good for you to get him checked out."

"But he's reached all his milestones," I said. "He claps, he talks, he points. Nobody's ever mentioned this before, not even his daycare provider."

Frank swatted the air. "It's probably nothing. We just thought we ought to mention it."

Probably nothing? How could it be nothing when I felt this sudden slam of heaviness? The very thought threatened to rip the picture of our lives into a thousand jagged pieces. Right now, one puzzle piece in particular nagged at me.

The previous weekend, I'd pushed Josiah's stroller through the glass tunnel aquarium at the Mall of America, and he'd acted out of character. While sharks and stingrays swam above and around him, Josiah seemed to look through them as if they were invisible. As if he couldn't see their bright colors, saucer-wide eyes, and round gaping mouths. To put it bluntly, the kid looked half-stoned.

*He's under the weather,* I'd told myself. The poor guy had just finished his second round of antibiotics from pinkeye that jumped from one eye to the other.

I glanced at my in-laws. "Look, if there's something wrong, we'd definitely want to know about it. Thanks for sharing. I'll be sure to get him checked out."

The next day, we dragged our tired bodies around the Children's Museum and made small talk about wooden blocks and optical illusions. On the outside, we looked like everybody else: a fun-loving, memory-making family. On the inside, however, thunder cracked.

As Josiah ran from place to place, climbing and hiding in a maze, my mind raced even faster. Another puzzle piece sprang to mind. Joey, the sweet redhead gal who ran Josiah's daycare, had recently told me that Josiah had been pulling kids' hair. I'd brushed the worry aside, chalking it up to another passing phase. Joey hadn't taken it seriously, so why should I? But the incident suddenly sparked new meaning. What if it meant something more?

My eyes darted like magnets, fastening to every long-haired little girl who could be a target for Josiah's eager fingers.

*Stop,* I scolded myself, *or this heightened awareness will drive you mad.*

I'd hoped this outing would prove my in-laws wrong and that Josiah would bounce back to his same old fun-loving self, but so far he hadn't. As long as I saw him through this new threatening lens, I couldn't help but scrutinize his every move. A big black box had been opened, and a host of ugly possibilities came tumbling out.

Josiah's doctor's appointment couldn't come fast enough. Dr. Roger had always leveled my mommy fears with his sage, good-natured advice. When Josiah was slow in learning to walk, the doctor gave him a thorough checkup and assured me he'd be fine, just fine.

"Everyone learns to walk at a different pace," he said. "Boys are slower to catch on, but I tell you what. If Josiah doesn't walk by the time he's twenty-four months, *then* we can worry."

A few weeks later, something clicked between Josiah's head and feet, and the little guy made up for lost time, leaving my worries in the dust, dozens of steps behind.

When I told Dr. Roger about my in-laws' recent observations, he spoke with his usual calmness. "Josiah looks fine. I don't yet have any real concerns. What do you say we give it another six months and check him then?"

"Or what?" I said. "What are my other options?"

"Well, I really don't think he needs it, but if it would help you feel better, why don't I go ahead and refer him to the Courage Center for more testing."

Over the next three weeks, Josiah spiraled downward—fast. His words began to disappear into thin air like smoke. Words we had worked on together. Words we had celebrated that brought his colorful personality to our world. Where did they go? And why did his eyes suddenly look so hollow and vacant, like someone had switched off his light? He faded in and out like a bulb with a loose connection. What was wrong with our son?

Grief-stricken, Joe and I quarantined ourselves in the house over Labor Day weekend, dragging around our bodies in a fog. Josiah kept flicking the lights on and off, on and off. He also repeatedly pushed buttons on his toys. *Beep, beep, beep.*

"Josiah, look at Mommy." I spider-tickled my fingers up his belly.

Nothing.

I poked my head under a blanket and stuck my face in front of his. Still no response. He stared into some kind of no man's land of blankness.

"Joe, he looks like he's been hijacked!"

Tissues couldn't hold my tears, so I buried my face in a towel and sobbed. How could the doctor have been so wrong? How could God let this happen to our child?

Josiah's testing at the Courage Center turned into therapy three times a week, but they still couldn't give us any concrete answers. Neither could the Early Childhood Intervention people who came over for in-home assessments.

Life became a balancing act as Joe and I took turns driving Josiah across town and back to daycare. Following each stint, we hightailed it back to our jobs having no clue when this high-speed spinning in circles would stop. What was wrong with our son?

At the end of September, Aneta, one of Josiah's more experienced therapists, offered the slightest puff of hope. "I really don't think Josiah has autism," she said.

I felt my face brighten. "You don't?"

"No. He doesn't present all the normal signs. I think it would be good to get his eyes and ears tested. Maybe it's something else."

My mind raced. Eyes and ears—of course. Why hadn't we thought of that? Everybody knows how hearing can throw a person off.

Armed with fresh hope, I drove Josiah to an ear, nose, and throat specialist in Maplewood. Josiah sat on my lap in an airtight room while snippets of faint sounds piped through internal wall speakers. Music, beeps, whispers, puffs, animal sounds, high-pitched whistles. Every time the sounds reached his ears, he turned in the direction they came from. Sadly, his ears worked fine.

On October fourth, we celebrated Josiah's second birthday by taking him to Stillwater to get his eyes tested. It offered only a slim thread of hope, but I held it like a lifeline.

A skinny girl led us to a quiet room, and I became Josiah's human straightjacket to harness his squirming body. When she sprayed dilating solution in his eyes, he cried, screamed, and flailed—all at the same time.

Thirty minutes later, the doctor tried to get Josiah's attention with a light-up spinner, while I did my best to protect my face from his thrashing head. The doctor held magnifiers in front of Josiah's eyes to see if his pupils would focus.

"Sorry to break this to you," he said, crossing his arms. "But your son is very far-sighted and needs glasses."

The eight hundred dollars we spent on two tiny pairs gave us more hope than we'd known in weeks.

As soon as we got home, I slipped those babies over his nose and tried to teach him to keep them on. "Here we go!" Holding his hands at his sides, I broke into song: "Row, row, row your boat, gently down the stream." We made it ten seconds before he ripped them off. "Good job, JoJo. Let's go a bit longer next time. Merrily, merrily, merrily, merrily. Life is but a dream."

I repeated this day and night—but still he wouldn't look at us.

After a week of working with him and the glasses, two of his therapists sat us down with grim faces. "We too were hopeful," one of them said. "But this is clearly more than a vision problem."

I went limp. Of course it was. My fears came flooding back.

"Mom, we're losing him," I cried into the phone.

Over the last several years, Mom had been a pillar to me, a woman of faith who knew exactly what to say and when. She lived miles away, but she might as well have lived across the street for all the closeness we shared.

"I know it's incredibly hard, honey."

I choked down a sob. "He's lost his words, he's become a picky eater, and he wakes up in the middle of the night with horrible night terrors. His eyes are open, but he can't snap out of his dreams. Mom, it's terrifying. He's a completely different kid."

"You'll get through this, beautiful. Josiah might be your baby, but you're my baby and I'm here for you. Let me pray."

When Dad passed away, I'd comforted Mom when she thought she couldn't go on. "Yes, you can," I assured her, "with God's help." I called her throughout the day to read Scripture, cry, and pray. I hugged her up and down with my words, reaching out to her like a hand gripping a feather. Now it was her turn to hammock me in God's strength.

"Father, send Tahni and Joe your peace and wisdom. Reveal anything hidden. Show them what to do next. Hold my little grandson close in your care. In Jesus' name."

After I hung up, I collapsed at the kitchen table where it had all begun three months before. *Where are you, God?*

I'd grown up in a Baptist church and school, even collected a little Holy Spirit fire along the way. I'd prayed for Josiah's protection since pregnancy: *Lord, cover this child under your wings. Make him or her a light to the nations.*

How could he be a light to the nations when he had a completely switched-off circuit?

# 2

# Worst Nightmare

"A jail of autism is no picnic."

– Josiah Cullen

**October 2007**

I hunkered under a blanket on my basement sectional, punching Josiah's symptoms into Google. *Please*, I thought, *anything but the A-word*. But it kept cropping up like bad apples on a slot machine.

I spent hours whipping through sites, then I found a video comparing a typical child with an autistic one. My body tightened as a therapist gave each child a candle, a pretend birthday cake, and a mound of Play-Doh. The typical child stuck the candle in the cake, but the autistic one aimlessly ground it into the Play-Doh.

"Typical kids learn through imitation," the narrator explained. "Children with autism don't know how to imitate or pretend. They have broken mirror neurons, which makes them lack social cues."

The workers gave the children a Big Bird doll, a cup, and a spoon. The typical child pretended to feed Big Bird, while the autistic one banged his spoon on the tray.

Tears burned my eyes as they handed the children little cars. The typical child played with the car, rolling it on the floor like Josiah used to do, but the autistic one spun the wheels in a way that looked all too familiar. Josiah had forgotten how to play with cars.

A mountain-sized weight pressed my heart, threatening to

crush me. I ran upstairs past the baskets of dirty laundry, past our smiling family wall portraits, past Josiah napping in his room, and stepped between Joe and his Sunday football game.

"Interception!" he cried, craning to see around me.

"Joe, I need to show you something. I know what's wrong with Josiah."

He followed me downstairs in silence, and I showed him the video with the clear-cut comparison. Neither of us could deny it. The child with autism acted just like Josiah.

Sadness cloaked Joe's eyes as he draped an arm over me and pulled me to his chest. When I stepped back, his eyes looked red and glassy. He tucked a strand of hair behind my ear. "Baby, we'll lick this." His usually strong base voice cracked. "We'll do whatever it takes to help our son."

Joe threw himself into autism research.

"I have an idea," he said, looking up from his laptop in the kitchen. "Jason, the sports blogger I follow, has a son with autism. I'll get in touch with him and ask questions."

Joe's blogger friend advised us to immerse Josiah in intensive therapy for six or seven hours a day. *The first five years are the most critical,* he wrote. *Kids with autism have a much better chance of improvement if you get them into the right program.*

Joe called around and found Partners in Excellence, a facility that offered full-time applied behavioral analysis therapy, and he set up a tour.

"This will be an adventure," I told Josiah.

Joe opened the door to the building, and seconds later, a lady with warm, soulful blue eyes extended her hand. "Hi, I'm Keri, the director. Please come in." Swiping her card, she unlocked a thick set of doors and ushered us into a room with a massive indoor trampoline and multiple shelves of toys. Play stations transformed the place into a large make-believe village, complete with a pretend doctor's office, kitchen, store, and school. Each station contained tall plastic bins and every kind of costume under the sun.

"We do everything we can to stir the child's imagination." Keri's tender voice lowered my stress level, but I still had to fight back tears. We'd dreamed of touring preschool buildings, not therapy centers.

Two smiley therapists stepped over to Josiah with kid-friendly gusto. "Ready to play?"

I couldn't believe what I saw next. Josiah walked away from us and took off with these complete strangers, without even looking back. What happened to the toddler who had recently battled separation anxiety? The boy who used to cry, "Mama, Mama," whenever we dropped him off at kids' church? What I wouldn't do to hear those persistent cries. My little JoJo. Did he even remember me? Of course he'd walk off with strangers. Why wouldn't he? He was already a thousand miles away.

Keri led us down a hall and cracked open a door. "This is our Bridges classroom. It's for kids preparing to transition to public kindergarten next year."

Their lively back-and-forth banter and happy-go-lucky ways reminded me of how Josiah used to be. If Partners therapists could help these kids, perhaps they could help Josiah too. And maybe he could even join their class someday.

Keri closed the door and led us through therapy swings, funny-looking jumpy things, and a winding maze of cubicles.

"Each of these spaces belongs to a child," she told us. "Each cubicle contains a small table, two plastic chairs, a shelf, and a pocket organizer with each child's favorite motivators. Children go to them several times a day for drills."

Joe's eyebrows shot up. "Drills? What do those involve?"

"Different things. For one, we teach using a reward system. The children match things to get a reward, label things to get a reward, and sort things to get a reward. It even works for washing their hands. They wet their hands to get a reward, lather for a reward, and rinse to get a reward."

Gosh, it sounded more like a dog-training academy. Reducing basic tasks to the tiniest ritualistic steps.

Keri patted my shoulder. "You have an advantage by sending him here early. Your two-year-old would be our youngest, but we'll pour ourselves into him and give him all the extra help he needs."

I could tell from Joe's face that she'd won him over.

"When can he start?" I asked.

"As soon as he has an official medical diagnosis for insurance."

Joe paced our living room. "This is nuts," he said. "I called the Alexander Center, the University of Minnesota, and Children's Hospital. Everybody has a waiting list between four months and a year."

"What should we do?" I asked.

"Well, I set up something with the Alexander Center because they had the shortest list, but I think we need a plan B."

That's when I found a qualified psychologist who agreed to come to our home, observe Josiah, and give him an official evaluation.

The white-haired man who made himself at home looked like he'd stepped out of the history books. He tested Josiah using little triangles for sorting and toy cars that looked like they'd been teleported from the fifties.

At the end of our visit he wanted me to complete a form that was so thick it could have passed for an SAT exam. Filling it out, I even needed a number two pencil to darken the circles.

When the expensive report finally arrived in the mail, I dissected the envelope with kid gloves, knowing these forms could be more detrimental to Josiah's future than a college rejection letter.

I eagerly flipped through, but when I came to the last line, I froze: Inconclusive for Autism Spectrum Disorder.

My voice trembled as I called the psychologist. "My son needs help as soon as possible, and the only way we can get him in our choice center is if you give him an official diagnosis. You say he doesn't present *all* the signs, but you saw for yourself that he shows most of them. Would you *please* reconsider and tell me my son has autism."

"Fair enough," he said, "I'll do it."

Only then did I exhale a thousand particles of stress.

Josiah jumped into Partners with both feet, and we felt a rush of fresh dreams and possibilities.

"Sweet boy," said Kim, a kind therapist in her early twenties. "We'll figure out what motivates him and move forward from there."

The therapists quickly learned he liked music. When Joe and I visited, we watched them sing "Take Me Out to the Ball Game" and "The Wheels on the Bus." We attended parent hour with the Pod 10 crew and befriended the parents of Josiah's young peer group. Since our old friends no longer knew how to relate to us, this came as a welcomed relief.

Kim smiled whenever she mentioned Josiah's efforts. She loved that boy, and I loved the bond they shared.

At parent meetings and trainings, therapists told us how hard Josiah worked. This could only mean one thing: we were on the right track and heading for a breakthrough.

After a month into Partners, the Alexander Center called. "We have an opening for Josiah's official evaluation." We already had a psychologist's official diagnosis, but we needed more clarity and professional certainty. A detailed analysis would explain the severity of Josiah's autism, and the doctors could give us medical direction and advice about what to expect in the future.

For two long days we saw medical and speech doctors, occupational therapists, and childhood development specialists. More professionals in white coats than angels in a Christmas play.

Joe and I sat beside our two-year-old and filled out copious paperwork. During breaks, we thanked God for portable DVD players and friends like Tanya, who earned the lifesaver-of-the-year award for watching Josiah and his endless Praise Baby videos.

At the end of the second day, they called us into the boardroom to share their findings. Five doctors gathered around the table while I tried to ignore the Kleenex box in the middle.

The pediatric psychologist cleared his throat and handed us a navy folder with three big words branded across the front: Autism Spectrum Disorder. So that was it. My son's assessment summed up in one big ugly label. My throat felt dry as I opened the cover.

They took turns giving us the lowdown on Josiah's assessments. His skills ranked painfully low. I saw places in the report that showed how kids his age had mastered certain skills where Josiah practically flat-lined. In some instances he dipped as low as a nine-month-old. Major gaps and lacks screamed at me in almost every skills category.

Whenever the men in white highlighted another gap, it took an elephant-sized bite out of my hopes. This had to be worse than getting straight Fs in college. Seeing your once-normal child's lack of abilities in black and white had a way of punching you in the gut and leaving you black and blue.

Joe looked them in the eyes. "We know he's delayed, but how bad do you think his autism is going to be?"

Their faces stayed cerebral as a medical doctor spoke up. "He's rather young to make that kind of prediction, but it's good you caught it early."

I squared back my shoulders. "You can't tell us anything more?"

A bearded doctor shook his head. "All we can really say about autism is that there's no known cause, no known cure, and it's lifelong."

His words felt like a prison sentence in a courtroom. "Isn't there anything else we can do? Like special diets and alternative medicine? I've done a little research on dairy-free, gluten-free diets. What about that whole biomedical approach?"

Their eyebrows shot up, and the medical doctor sighed. "That's old folk wisdom. I'm not going to tell you how to spend your money, but those findings are purely anecdotal and experiential. Parents report the same thing with placebos. If I were you, I wouldn't waste my money on any of that jazz. Keeping him at Partners is good though."

The others nodded while the medical doctor crossed his arms as if he'd saved the day.

When I collapsed into the car beside Joe, I noticed a pamphlet sticking out of the folder they gave me, so I pulled it out. What? Identification bracelets for kids with autism? You mean they expected these kids to run away and this special bracelet was supposed to help us find them? I threw it on the floor and stomped on it. If what those doctors said was true, it would take a whole lot more than a bracelet to bring him back.

Joe reached for my hand as we drove home in silence. I glanced at Josiah whose breathing slowed as he drifted into slumber land.

*My beautiful boy. How I wish I could trade places with you …*

His eyes moved back and forth behind his lids. Where did he go under those clear pools of blue that used to brighten whenever he saw us? After naptime, I'd kiss his pale plump cheeks and tell him, "It's time to play, sweet bear." Now whenever he woke up, he pulled us into an entirely different world.

The wind picked up against our Corolla, and our forty-minute trek across the metro felt like a trip to the cemetery to bury our dreams.

I thought of when Dad died. He had just finished one of Mom's home-cooked meals, sat with her on the couch, dangled his arm around her, and said, "I think we need to call the doctor."

Mom stepped out for a second, and when she returned she found him collapsed on the floor. Minutes later, he died in the ambulance. Fast, and without warning.

I grieved deep, but in time, I'd moved on. This beast called autism, however, threatened to torment me indefinitely. "I'll make your life crazy difficult," it hissed. "No matter where you go, I'll be right there in the backseat following you."

Was this ongoing death really my new reality?

Goodbye future proms and teaching my son how to drive. I might as well forget about someday meeting his future wife. And so much for grandchildren.

Looking ahead, I only saw loss upon loss, uncertainties on every side, and a son who could be mostly oblivious to all of it.

## 3

# The Race Is On

"Talking is hard for me. Men are meant to talk."

– Josiah Cullen

*January 2008*

Joe and I slumped in a café near Partners like two drowning souls trying to yank each other out of the water.

"We're gonna make it, Tahni. We're doing everything we can."

Joe's blogger friend had been right about the importance of intervention in the first five years, but the narrowing window only made the urgency breathe down our necks with extra intensity.

Joe sipped his cherry smoothie and shook his head. "Sorry you had a rough morning with Josiah's urine sample fiascos."

He knew my routine. At night I had to pin the boy on his bed, wrap a sticky sponge around his privates, and connect him to the pee bag in his diaper. Then, at the crack of dawn, I had to awaken him to collect it all. The doctor said the urine test would tell us if his body had chemical, viral, or environmental pollutants causing inflammation and chronic illness.

But this morning Josiah had done it again. He'd flailed and twisted his wiry body in such a way that he leaked urine into his diaper, precisely where it wasn't supposed to go. That meant I had the fun job of extracting every last bit of it from the sponge only to discover since the amount didn't reach the magic line on the vial, the entire test was a failure.

"There's always tomorrow," I told Joe with mock enthusiasm. "If we complete the kit, we can be done with this. Stick the sample in an envelope, pay the seventy bucks, and FedEx his pee to France. I still don't understand why their labs are better than ours, but oh well."

Joe sniffed a laugh. "You know what I think, babe. We need more drama in our lives."

Now it was my turn to laugh. Joe and I had been involved in drama since college. Our mutual interest in acting had brought us to work at Fort Abraham Lincoln, where we gave tours as living history interpreters. Joe dressed up as a soldier and I as an army laundress. Our worlds converged and revolved around drama and communications. Oddly enough, they still did. Only now, our dramas revolved around our son who could *not* communicate.

I downed the last of my bagel and milk, two foods Josiah couldn't eat, since kids with autism often suffered from digestion issues. According to Josiah's Defeat Autism Now (DAN) doctor, his "leaky gut" wreaked havoc on his immune system. The doctor wanted to detoxify him and rescue him from all those pesky little cellular terrorists.

Turmeric, calcium, zinc, fish oil, vitamin D3, and olive leaf extract. We gave him all these goodies and more. You name it, we threw it in the blender into some kind of smoothie. "Drink up, JoJo. It's good for you."

Good for him, brutal on our bank account. DAN doctors weren't covered by insurance, so Josiah's treatments and office visits cost between six and eight hundred dollars a month. Not an easy pill to swallow on a conservative budget. Unfortunately, the treatments didn't work as well as we'd hoped, so the DAN doctor suggested we consult a medical doctor and start giving Josiah vitamin B12 shots.

I'll never forget how I stood in the kitchen with a syringe in my hand, casting a helpless look at Joe. "I don't know if I can do this without practicing."

"You can practice on me," he offered.

A smile crept across my face. "Sure. Good idea."

"Wait. I was kidding."

"Well, I'm not."

He let out a tired sigh and rubbed the back of his neck. "Trust me. It's a bad idea."

"Listen, Joe. If a three-year-old can do it, I'm sure you're old enough to do it too."

He looked like a kid at his first dentist appointment. "Um ... how about we forget I just said anything? You'll be fine."

"Too late. You've already committed yourself." I chased him to the bedroom.

"All right," he said, panting. "Let's get this over with."

I squeezed the syringe. "Remember, you're doing this for JoJo. Okay, bend over and show me a bare butt cheek."

He gritted his teeth. "Are you sure you don't want to practice on a stuffed animal?"

"No, they don't feel pain. Hold still."

"Ouch!"

"You okay?"

He puffed out his chest. "Ha. Actually, I barely felt it."

I gave him a kiss. "Sorry I don't have a lollipop. Thanks."

Armed with fresh confidence, I tiptoed to Josiah's room and stood in his doorway. Of course, he didn't look up. Scooping him in my arms, I dragged the two of us to his diaper-changing table and rolled him on his belly.

"JoJo, we've found another way to give you vitamins. It just involves a little poke. Are you ready?" I did it so fast that he didn't even flinch.

How sad that it never helped though.

The biomedical approach had been trial and error from day one. The diet had only slightly improved his brain fog and loose stools. It certainly didn't help with his speech. The same applied to the B12 shots. With the looming five-year window, the dark shades over my own foggy brain only kept creeping lower.

Pain followed me wherever I went, even to Target. As I stood in line, a little attention-seeking girl flirted at me with her eyes—and it worked.

"I'm this many," she said, holding up four fingers. "For my birthday my mommy bought me a dolly with really long hair, except you can't cut it because then she'd be ugly."

*Such a fascinating creature*, I mused. *So full of life.*

"I pretend I'm her babysitter," she said. "And ... and when I tuck her in at night, I always make sure she says her prayers 'cause she's a-scared of the dark."

Her mother drew her in close. "She's a talker, this one."

I smiled, holding back tears.

As the days dragged on, I devoured every book, video, and article I could find on autism. I discovered that a TV personality with an autistic son used a hyperbaric oxygen chamber. At this point, I'd try anything, and since one of our biomedical doctors had recently added a soft-sided hyperbaric chamber to her practice, I eyed the long inflated tube during our next visit.

"Wow, it's small," I said. "Both my son and I can fit inside?"

"Yes, and you can even watch a video or read a book," she said.

"Mind if I step inside?"

"Be my guest." She unzipped the capsule and I lowered myself into the tube that felt like a cross between a tanning bed and a casket. It would work great in a horror flick because it hit three big phobias at once: confinement in tight places, loud noises, and being buried alive.

I wrestled with the chamber decision for weeks. Then one day at Partners, when I found myself missing Kim, Josiah's old favorite therapist who'd left to pursue her education, I struck up a conversation with Jeni, the mother of one of Josiah's peers.

"We recently leased a soft-sided machine for Ben," she said. "It's set up in our kitchen. We live in Wisconsin, but you're welcome to come see if Josiah can handle it—before you cough up all that money."

So we took Jeni up on her offer. When Josiah handled it really well, I talked to Joe, and we decided to check out a clinic with a hard-sided model. The time and expense would be huge, but the possibility of helping Josiah regain his words would be worth it.

When we arrived for our first dive, the technician crouched to Josiah's level. "Hey, big guy, I need to measure your neck so we can fit you in one of these nifty-looking oxygen hoods. We're going to pump it up with pure oxygen and make you look like a space man."

An attendant climbed in with us. When he covered Josiah's head with the hood, I tried to hold it together. How in the world would Josiah keep that thing on his head for a whole hour? If he ripped it off, the whole treatment would be ruined.

"Let's fasten you into your seat," he said.

I started to sing, "We all live in a blue submarine, a blue submarine, a blue submarine ..."

The attendant pointed at two holes in the side of the tube. "You can watch videos through these."

"Hear that, JoJo? Videos."

I prayed as they started the machine, and I couldn't believe it. Two minutes into it Josiah fell asleep. His head, confined in that clear plastic hood, dropped to the side while drool dripped down.

Finally the machine gave its last groan, and I breathed a sigh of relief. One dive down, thirty-nine to go. From what I'd read, improvement could come right away, but for some people it didn't start until after about twenty dives.

By session thirty, worry set in. I'd been looking for the tiniest sparks of progress. Josiah slept a bit better and seemed to look at us a little more, but where were his words? Where was the "Mama, Mama"?

*Hang in there,* I told myself. *You still have ten treatments to go. That means ten more times to oxygenate those cells and regenerate the paths of healing.*

When our last treatment came and went with still no words, the doctor looked at me. "Would you like to try forty more dives?"

I left feeling deflated and defeated. We'd depleted everything to get to this dead-end street, and had nothing left to give, nothing left to do. Clearly, we needed a miracle.

One night my back hurt and I had trouble sleeping, so I grabbed Josiah's old baby journal and began to read.

*February 4, 2006*

*Josiah, you are saying a lot of words now. Mama, Daddy, juice, cheese, no-no, bawk-bawk (for chicken), JoJo, banana, cookie, bumblebee, buzz, good, yay, and horse.*

*You love books, especially ones with bananas, cheese, and chickens.*

*We went to the mall a couple weeks ago and got one of the mall strollers. It had a steering wheel, so you had one hand steering and the other arm resting over the side. You thought you were hot stuff. You were so good the whole time.*

*Grandma and Grandpa were here visiting for a few days before their trip to Hawaii. You saw them and gave them nice hugs. You had a lot of fun showing them all your tricks.*

*You're humming your own little tunes now.*

*Love you, my little angelic boy!*

*I know you're not going to be little for long, so I'm savoring every snuggle, cuddle, and nuzzle.*

Dimming the light, I hugged the book to my chest. I didn't even try to stop the tears.

*God, why didn't you come through for me with all these treatments? How could you let this happen? If you're out there, I need to feel you again. Please, I beg you.*

# 4

# Sensing God

"Miles make you joyful in the little things
to befriend the biggest adventure."

– Josiah Cullen

**August 2008**

I dragged my sleep-deprived body to my unmade bed and collapsed like a ragdoll. Autism had wiped me out, and God felt a million miles away. Sleep screamed for me, and I ached to escape this lonely exhaustion.

With Joe out running errands and Josiah passed out on the couch after another sleepless night, I seized this golden opportunity for a nap. Breathing deep, I crashed into a pool of dreams.

Suddenly, I jerked awake.

My nose twitched and my heart quickened. What was that smell? A most amazing fragrance, captivating and rich.

I glanced at my clock. Strange. It wasn't even four p.m. I'd slept less than half an hour. What kind of smell could wake me up like that? Where had it come from, and how could it pump me with so much joy?

Burnt vanilla? Cinnamon? Crème brulée? My mind twirled and swirled as I flitted around my room like a bloodhound, squinting, sniffing, eager to figure this out. Had it come from my pillowcase? No. My sheets? No. My hair? That wasn't it either.

I darted to my window and checked my neighbor's dryer vent, but no, I didn't see even the slightest trace of exhaust. Was I losing my mind?

I dashed to the hall. No smell out there. I hurried back to my bed, and for the next twenty minutes, I drew in long succulent breaths. Then it lifted.

Wait. Hadn't my mom experienced something similar when my dad died? Mom had been visiting my brother in Arizona when she awoke to an intense smell. The fragrance of the Lord, she called it.

I hurried to the kitchen to grab my laptop and google *presence of the Lord, vanilla,* and *cinnamon smells.* My eyes widened as I scrolled through websites that told of others who experienced this same phenomenon.

Then it struck me. I had been stuck in a cave of stinky thinking before the fragrance came. I thought God had abandoned me. But this? Had he really just given me a supernatural manifestation in the form of a sensory experience? Yes, I believed he had. By soaking me with the richness of his presence, he reminded me that he hadn't forgotten me. He'd walked right in my room and helped me feel him as close as the air I breathed. Because of all my hurt, I had put up walls around my heart, but God leaked through to show me he'd never left me. *He* wasn't the one who walked away, and now I knew with certainty he never would.

The fragrance had lifted, but the potent truth of God's presence remained, settling on me with peaceful stillness.

*Thank you, God, for reaching into my dark space when I couldn't feel you. Thank you for fanning the flames of my faith and awakening me to the assurance of your presence.*

### February 2010

For two long years, Joe and I tried various treatments for our now four-year-old son, but nothing delivered even the slightest improvement with his ongoing developmental delays.

After experiencing the fragrance of the Lord, however, I studied the Bible with fresh intensity. To help me get through, God led me to Michele, a lady from church who had a son with autism. We gravitated toward each other like moths hungry for the light.

One chilly day, I burst into Michele's house. "Guess what? I found an online video about a woman whose son God healed of autism!"

She lit up. "I've got to see this."

"The lady attends a big church in Redding, California," I said. "I watched her pastor's sermon on YouTube and bawled. He showed from Scripture that God wants to heal the sick, raise the dead, cast out devils, and cleanse lepers. He says we're not supposed to make up theologies or excuses about why people don't get healed—because Jesus, by his actions, is already our perfect theology."

"Oh, you're talking about Bethel Church. I love their worship songs. Hey, I wonder if they offer conferences or anything. We should check it out."

I laughed. "Yeah, and take a trip to Paris while we're at it."

But as much as I tried, I couldn't get Michele's wacky idea out of my head. That's when I went online and discovered that Bethel offered an evangelism conference in just three weeks. A conference that trained and liberated both seasoned and timid believers to demonstrate the kingdom of heaven through love and power.

*Get real, Tahni,* I told myself. *Josiah's bills are hanging over your head like a noose. How could you possibly leave Josiah with Joe for several days in a row?*

Ignoring all sound reasoning, I sent Michele the information anyway.

She replied in a few hours: "Let's pray about it, ask our husbands, and see if God gives us a green light."

It felt like a dream when Michele and I found ourselves in California sitting through our first session. Joe had told me, "Don't worry. Your hunky husband can handle this." So here we were.

"We need to take risks and step out in authority," said the conference leader. "Quit living defensively. You have the ball, so get up and be glorious. Your light has come!"

Before lunch he encouraged us to go into the marketplace and ask God to highlight people he wanted us to reach out to. That's when I felt my appetite go away, even as we headed to a Chinese restaurant.

When we sat at a table with our little group, Michele and I exchanged nervous glances. What if people thought we were part of a cult or something?

A young Asian waitress stepped up. "Ready to order?"

We told her what we wanted, and one of the gals, Sunneye, switched the topic and began telling the waitress beautiful things God felt about her, even personal details about her life.

"H-how did you know all this?" the waitress asked.

Sunneye pointed upward. "The Lord knows. He simply uses me to share his memos."

The woman wiped her eyes. "Well, I'm a single mother, trying to work and go to school at the same time. It's been very hard, but you make me feel so understood."

We gave her a big tip and felt like a million bucks as we left for our next adventure at a strip mall.

When we stepped inside, Michele and I tried to look natural as we stood on the sidelines watching Sunneye and Kim casually engage shoppers with a warm "hello." They prayed for a young guy with a knee injury, and when he bent his leg back and forth, he told them the pain had all left. My faith soared. You mean ordinary people like us could just step up to strangers, love on them, and pray for them on the spot?

The next day, when a few of us walked through the double-doors of Walmart, something told me this would be my biggest stretch yet. Our leader had asked us to draw a picture we could give to someone God led us to on this "treasure hunt."

After our group split up, I fumbled in my purse for my picture. Just then, a woman stepped in front of me, and I couldn't believe my eyes. The back of her shirt had a river with squiggly lines and rocks—just like the ones in my picture!

*God, if this is the person I'm supposed to talk to, you're going to have to show me what to say.*

"Excuse me?" I said, breaking into a sweat.

She looked at me with questioning eyes, and I tried to look like I did this every day as I unfolded my drawing.

"This may sound strange," I said, "but I'm on a treasure hunt with some friends and I think you're the treasure. Before I came here, I drew this and it looks just like the picture on your shirt." I held it in front of her, feeling more like a fool by the second.

"You drew this?"

I nodded. "Would you mind if I told you what I think the picture might mean?"

"Sure, why not?"

I sucked in a breath and told her how I felt religion, with all its rules and rigidity, had started to erode the banks of her river. "Wherever God's river flows, there's life," I said. "Where religion has hurt you, God wants to free you." I exhaled. "Does that mean anything to you?"

Her eyebrows shot up. "Yes, it does."

"Really? I mean—great! Would you mind if I prayed for you?"

"Nah, I'm good."

Despite the fact she said no, I walked away on a cloud because—I'd heard from God! I didn't need him to ring a bell and say, "Attention. This is God speaking." I just needed to step in the water and watch him part it.

After we returned to the conference, the speaker shared an idea about getting so filled with God that we leaked him wherever we set our feet. He spoke of an uninhibited, unabashed joy that sounded as foreign to me as it did wonderful.

During ministry time, people kept approaching my friend Michele to pray for her. *Why her and not me?* I wondered. *When would I receive one of these special messages?* In case God had forgotten, I still needed him to heal Josiah's autism, not to mention my aching back.

Just then, a big guy started toward me. My pulse quickened. Clearly, God heard the cry and sent him in the right direction.

"I have a word for you," he said.

"Go ahead," I said, closing my eyes in utter expectancy.

"Do you have bunions on your feet?"

My eyes popped open. "Excuse me?" "Yes, but …"

"Well, God just showed me about that, so I'd like to pray for you."

Seriously? Couldn't the Lord do better than that? Exactly what was this? Some kind of cruel cosmic joke? My bunions barely bothered me, and frankly, I didn't care to discuss them with a stranger.

As he prayed his hearty prayer and I felt like a flat tire, I opened my eyes a pinch, and guess what I saw? Michele. She stood in the corner, getting prayed for—again. She had such a big smile on her face, she looked like she'd won the lottery.

Needless to say, as the conference drew to a close, I had a little talk with God. *Lord, Michele keeps getting all these amazing words, but I only heard about bunions. Could you please send someone to give me a serious word? An encouraging one maybe?*

Just then, a staff member tapped me on the shoulder. "Hi. God just prompted me to give you this gift."

"Really?"

I'm sure I looked stunned as she handed me a shiny red quarter-sized heart made of glass. "In the last five years, I've only given away four of these," she said, "but the Holy Spirit wanted me to give this one to you."

I could hardly speak. As she told me of God's unique love for me, a tear rolled down my face. As a recovering perfectionist and over-achiever, I made things more difficult than they had to be—even God's free gift of love. Sure, I had no problem telling God how much I loved *him*, but when it came to receiving his love, that's where I stumbled. My earthly father had hugged me a lot, but he didn't know how to open up and communicate with me. This left me with love deficits. Slivers in my soul.

In our final session, the speaker talked about an orphan mindset, and I realized that had been me before the conference—but not anymore. Worship started, and my back hurt as I raised my hands and belted out the songs with joy. Then the worship leader asked us to sing from Jesus' perspective.

"Tahni, you are beautiful, you are worthy, and I love you." Tears streamed down my face as God's truth saturated my dry, desperate places.

*God, thank you for helping me experience your love as a two-way street. It's not just me declaring it to you. It's you declaring it to me!*

We closed with a song about Jesus' power resurrecting all my dead hopes and dreams.

Lightened by everything that had happened during the conference, Michele and I couldn't stop laughing as we carried out our bags to the rental car.

"God, you love us," I shouted.

"We want to jump in your river!" cried Michele.

I wiggled my back and stopped short.

"What is it?" asked Michele.

"It doesn't hurt nearly as much," I said. "The Healer has already begun his good work."

# 5

# Slam

> "Turn love out of guaranteed doors."
>
> – Josiah Cullen

**November 2010**

As Joe and I sat on the blue and orange chairs in the Partners conference room, we waited with a mix of dread and hope. This was it. We'd come to the end of the five-year window.

I drew in a breath, inhaling the savory smell of meat from the Crock-Pots in the employee breakroom.

"Thanks for the dinner invite," quipped Joe.

Every six to eight weeks, we gathered around this conference table for a detailed analysis of Josiah's progress. They started with a video to show us how Josiah's good behavior had earned him a bounce on the trampoline with his dear friend, Emma.

"He's such a charmer," said Kristin, his primary therapist. "Just listen to his infectious laughter. Emma adores him."

Nicole, the senior therapist, chuckled. "He plays it so cool around her—but wait until another boy shows up. That changes everything."

I looked out the window at the construction site across the street and thought about Josiah experiencing his own kind of construction. Then I thought about our last conversation with Kim before she left Partners. During that meeting, she'd pointed out a blue jay on the windowsill. Here one moment, gone the next.

A million emotions had risen and fallen between these walls. Keri, the director, slid in front of us a copy of Josiah's report, reams of data neatly distilled into multi-colored bar graphs.

The therapists kept a bird's-eye view on these kids and took copious notes for their manual records. In addition, the staff wore clickers on their belt loops, tracking the kids' every move. Only God himself could have watched them more closely.

I scanned the papers, and my heart sank. Josiah's numbers and percentages couldn't be lower. After three years of therapy, he still ended up at the bottom percentile for his age range. Numbers like 6 percent and under assaulted my eyes, and each description pressed like a weight.

One comment read, *Josiah continues to present with significant sensory delays that have impacted his ability to maintain optimal arousal for participation in functional tasks.*

How could this be? His skills sounded more limited than ever.

Nicole read my face. "We really don't know how much Josiah is understanding about what we're saying these days." She glanced at Keri. "We think we should put a hold on the verbal speech work and switch our focus to picture communication."

What? Stop working on his verbal skills? That had been our main goal. Tears burned my eyes.

"We're sorry," Keri said. "You guys are awesome parents. We've watched you put everything into this. I don't think we've ever seen parents try as hard as the two of you."

Even with her soft tone, her words felt like bricks. In one fell swoop, our dreams crashed on the rocks. So much for him being like the kids in the Bridges program getting ready for public school. With reports like these, he couldn't be any less qualified.

My mind flip-flopped back to my own grade school days when I'd received my report cards. Anything less than an A made me crumble. At least back then good efforts determined great results. Not so with autism.

*You failed, Tahni. Failed the most important test. And there isn't a single thing you can do, because you'll never bring your little boy back.*

I happened to know that the kids of several of my friends had received favorable reports. It wasn't fair. They hadn't even given it a fraction of our efforts. We'd run ourselves ragged jumping through every possible hoop—and what did we have to show for it? Nothing but an empty bank account.

Sue, the psychologist, ran a hand through her red hair. "It's been a full-speed sprint for you guys, but autism is really more like a marathon." She grabbed a piece of paper and drew a huge curve. "This is what learning looks like for the typical child." She drew again. "And this is what it looks like for a child with autism."

I stared at the hairball of lines scribbled all over and had a hard time swallowing.

"Don't miss the joy of parenting your son," she said. "Play with him, have fun with him, do what he loves to do. Yes, you'll feel waves of grief, so please call us. We're always here for you."

"JoJo has a lot more life in him," Kristin added. "He could end up surprising us all someday."

But none of this encouragement from our second family was strong enough to hoist me out of my pit. We'd been praying Josiah would be able to join the "moderate" to "high-functioning" autism category, but now, at the end of our five-year window, he sounded as stuck as quicksand in the "severe" and "low-functioning" category.

Use picture communication instead of working toward speech? That wasn't even on the docket.

When Joe and I had noticed Josiah's fascination with Joe's iPod Touch, the previous year, we had done a little research. That's when we found Proloquo2Go, a communication app that uses symbols and speaks words aloud. Desperate to try anything that might help with his communication, we preordered an iPad.

And when it came we introduced the iPad and apps to Partners, hoping it might help others. Then we watched it replace the Velcro picture card system for labeling and making basic requests. God let us be pioneers in introducing this new invention to other families. However, those computerized words and pictures were only supposed to be fillers while we waited for Josiah to get his words back. Picture communication was supposed to be our starting point—not our miserable end.

Nicole spoke up. "I know this is extremely difficult, but we're saying these things for a good reason. We don't know how much he's even grasping what we're telling him these days. Don't worry though. When it comes to picture communication, we won't leave him where he's at. We hope to advance him beyond just pushing a picture for the word *cookie*. We'll help him learn how to push the *I want* button first. The same is true for bathroom requests and everything else."

Cookie, bathroom … Forget simple requests. What about knowing my son's thoughts and feelings?

Joe and I could no longer hold back the tears.

"Sorry," I said, wiping my face. "You guys have tried your best. Thank you."

What else could I say? We'd been chasing the wind to help him regain his speech, and now we'd come to a breathless dead end.

Desperate to make the best of this, I signed up for a one-day autism conference in River Falls, Wisconsin.

And as I drove with a new mother from Partners, a doctor, she looked at me with blood-shot eyes. "I just don't know how this could have happened. You take care of yourself your whole pregnancy. You do all the right things and—bam. You get sucker-punched with autism."

"I'm sorry," I said. "I understand."

I listened to her emote for an hour, identifying and remembering.

When we arrived at the University of Wisconsin, we circled around half a dozen times looking for a parking spot, but the ones near the main building had been taken, so we had to park a distance away.

"Sorry," I told her," as we sidestepped icy mounds of snow in the frigid weather. "If I'd known this, I would have warned you to bring your snow boots and parka."

We shivered like Eskimos as we stepped in, but I felt hopeful about learning new techniques in an optional breakout session called "Activities for the Non-Verbal Student."

Three speakers took the platform, and told us they'd mostly worked with kids over fourteen. Oh well. At least it could help me down the road.

They dimmed the lights and showed a home video of a real class in session with more than a dozen teenagers.

"This group represents three categories," the lady speaker said, over-enunciating her words. "Non-verbal, low-functioning, and intellectually disabled. Many of these non-verbal students with autism have a much harder time learning functional skills than students who just have intellectual disabilities."

I tensed.

"Our mentally challenged students actually do quite well practicing potential job skills like sorting nuts and bolts. Some can even do sweeping, cleaning, and grocery bagging. When it comes to students with severe and low-functioning autism, however, we feel we're doing great if we can just teach them a few functional skills like crushing cans and shredding paper."

Air. I had to fight to breathe.

"These non-verbal teens need a lot of predictable scheduled activities to keep them from hurting themselves and others. You need to watch them because if they get frustrated, they can escalate fast. They're strong when they reach puberty. We've seen teens put their heads through glass and their fists through sheetrock. So stay on the lookout if there's too much or too little sensory input. You need to learn how to quiet them down and help them redirect their aggressive energy."

The room swirled.

The teacher in the video gave her students a large box of rocks to pass over their heads. The box went around and around from one teen to next.

"Careful," she said as if talking to toddlers. "Good job!"

My heart sank. How could they make these teens do such juvenile, futile activities? It was one thing to think about your child not being able to drive or go to the prom. Quite another thing to imagine this kind of nightmare.

As the teens practiced more "activities," Josiah's upcoming years flashed before me. I hadn't processed the fact that he might be non-verbal for the rest of his life—and now I was supposed to accept that he might not be able to learn how to do practical things? He might not even be able to control himself? *Crushing cans, shredding paper.* The words replayed in my mind like a siren until I couldn't take it anymore. I jumped to my feet and ran to the restroom to weep.

*God, these beautiful trapped children … It's so horrible to see them like this. You promised your children a future and a hope. I'm going to hold you to that, God. Because no matter what happens— that will not be my son!*


When I got home, I shared about the autism conference with my support group, a handful of mothers from Partners who met on a regular basis. I loved this group. While mothers of typical children often went into crisis mode when Billy and Susie didn't get straight A's or make the dance team, these mothers functioned on a completely different wavelength.

During an early meeting, one mother had expressed her feelings about this. "I hate that kind of crap!" she said.

"Me too," another chimed in. "Hey, that's it. We should call ourselves the CRAP group. Coffee Relations for Autistic Parents." And that's how we started.

When the CRAP group heard about my experience, they wanted to cheer me up, so Jennifer invited us to her craftsman-style home to watch a documentary called *A Mother's Courage.*

Danette and I took the couch, Lesley eased into the armchair, and Jennifer perched on the kitchen barstool from where she served us scones, orange juice, and fruit.

I'd never heard of *A Mother's Courage* and sat mesmerized.

When doctors told a lady from Iceland that her non-verbal, severely autistic son had the mind of a toddler and couldn't understand anything, she refused to accept their negativity. Instead, she traveled abroad on a quest for knowledge about how to connect with these kids. I was familiar with all the basic techniques and therapies she encountered—until she talked about meeting Soma from India.

Soma's knowledge came from working with her severely autistic son, Tito. Soma threw everything into his education and finally experienced a major communication breakthrough. Eager to share it with others, she opened a center to help severely autistic children learn how to spell.

I watched in amazement as step by step Soma communicated with each child using her personally invented technique called the Rapid Prompting Method, or RPM. Children like Josiah could point at letters and actually spell words! With darting eyes and jerking bodies, their fingers pointed letter by letter at simple plastic stencils. Soma talked to them as if they were smart, and they actually lived up to it!

Jennifer wiped her eyes. "Isn't this incredible?"

"Unreal," I said. "I need to know more about this."

6

# Open Door

"Peace bounces like a ball. Put up peace
into your net if you wish to score."
– Josiah Cullen

After I had worked at Eagle Brook Church for almost ten years, Pastor Bob announced that we'd be expanding to a few new campuses. They would simulcast the pastor's message live from the main campus across the metro. Each location would need both a campus pastor and a ministry director—someone to oversee staff and ministries, mobilize volunteers, and care for attendees.

Naturally, with this massive restructure, I wondered what would happen to my specialized role of directing promotional communications. On my blog lately, I'd been encouraging moms and dads of autistic children. Not only did I love this kind of outreach, but it awakened in me a stronger desire to make a difference in people's lives. Could this church expansion possibly be God's way of nudging me in a new direction, perhaps one involving ministry on the front lines?

I thought back to when we moved to the Twin Cities from North Dakota, and I took a job at a performing arts place called Theatre De La Jeune Lune. Eighteen months later, I'd felt this same unsettled feeling, and God used it to nudge me into ministry at Eagle Brook. Was it time to step through an entirely new door?

I talked and prayed about it with Joe. Then I set up an appointment with the executive pastor, my old boss, Scott.

When I settled across from him at his desk, I went right to my point. "With all the changes, should I be looking for a new job?"

Scott shook his head. "I don't know where we'll put you, but you're a fabulous employee and we don't want to lose you."

"Well, I've been going through this autism journey for quite some time now, and God has been doing a lot of work in my spiritual life. During my time on staff, I've been studying Scripture and learning. So I guess what I'm trying to say is … would you consider me for a position on the ministry side of things?"

"Really?" he said, adjusting his glasses. He pulled out a folder and plunked it in front of me. "We do still need ministry directors at two of our new campuses, Spring Lake Park and White Bear Lake. Would you consider working at one of those?"

"Sure. I mean yes. I'd love to be a ministry director at Spring Lake Park. That's where Pastor Steve is, and I highly respect him. I'd love to learn under his leadership."

He leaned back. "Okay. I'll see if Steve and the others agree, but I think you'd be a great fit. We just need you to fill out the application and statement of faith and get you in front of the board. After you're hired, we'll give you several months of training, and then you can apply for your pastor's license."

Joe got a kick out of the idea of me being called "Pastor Tahni." But he gave me his full support, even knowing our schedule would be anything but normal.

And when God gave me the job and everything fit into place, I jumped into my new position with both feet.

I cherished my Spring Lake Park pastoral team, and I loved being available to people at all the services. Twenty-five hundred people came to our campus, and many approached me on Sundays with their thoughts, needs, and feelings.

"How did you know what to pray for me?" one woman asked. "I never even told you about it."

"As we step out in love," I said, "the Lord leads."

I learned to pray for people on the spot rather than just saying I'd pray for them later. The more I ventured out, the more God reminded me what he'd shown me at Bethel. He wants to speak to all of us. We just need to learn how to hear his voice.

Shortly after receiving my pastor's license, Kriste, my seventeen-year-old niece called at three in the morning, sobbing. "Aunt Tahni?"

"What's wrong, honey?"

"It's Daddy. He's gone!"

I froze, trying to swallow. My forty-seven-year-old brother? No! It didn't make sense. I knew he'd been struggling with an infection—but this? *Dean, why didn't you go to the doctor?*

I'd loved my big biker brother with all his tattoos and black leather. He was tough, but had a soft heart of gold. Everyone loved his sidesplitting sense of humor. How could he be gone just like that?

The next thing I knew, I found myself standing at a podium in front of my family and hometown friends. How had I come to officiate my first memorial for my own brother? Because when Mom asked, I couldn't say "no." I started by sharing about his other memorial service in Arizona.

"One of Dean's friends called him a very big man, but he wasn't just talking about size. He called Dean a big blanket and invited people to look around the room at the hundreds of lives Dean had touched. Sadly, because of his appearance, Dean wouldn't have been accepted in many churches. But in the way he loved, he looked a lot like Jesus. We can touch lives like that too. In the little time we're given, how do we do it?

"Are we living with tightly closed fists, always grasping for ourselves, or are we living with hands wide open, ready to dish out a little hope?

"You may believe in God. You may like Jesus. You may have acknowledged him at some point. But have you made him Lord? The step is pretty simple, really. You can just say in your heart, 'God I'm tired of doing this on my own. I sin. I mess up. I don't get it right, and I need you. I need your Son, Jesus, to come into my life, to forgive me and by his Spirit, make me whole. I accept your Son who died for me. I accept your gift of eternity in heaven and your supernatural guidance on earth. You are Lord, and I want to follow you.'

"Dean was by no means perfect," I concluded. "But I can tell you this: he took that step. That's why we don't grieve without hope. And I know something else. Dean wants to see you with him in heaven someday."

I drove to the cemetery in silence, remembering all too well this same long gravel road half a mile out of town. They divided the cemetery property into two parts, one for Protestants and one for Catholics. Thank God we'd all be together in heaven, so long as we believed in Christ.

The wind picked up, tossing dirt in the air as I gathered close with family and friends on the hilltop.

There, I peered over the flatlands of South Dakota, the endless stretch of faded greenery dotted with houses and small buildings. Countless stories lay nestled in this town of six hundred. And a thousand family memories lay tucked beneath a sweeping sea of tombstones with names carved in shadows: Grandpa Rusty, Grandma Mary, Grandpa John, Grandma Alma, Auntie, and of course, my beloved daddy. Mom's name and birth year were already engraved beside his, punctuated with an open-ended dash. I hugged Mom and my other brother, Shane.

A portion of Dean's ashes would join Daddy's, and life would go on. Whenever thinking about Dean, we'd try our best to imagine him laughing it up in heaven with the other relatives.

Staring at death never grew easier. I certainly didn't expect to face it again a few months later.

Pastor Steve and I had been regularly checking on little two-month-old Gracie in the hospital. One day, when Pastor Steve's adult son suddenly passed away, I really didn't think anything worse could go wrong. But it did. Gracie died the next day.

I'd never felt so helpless as when I sat in the sterile room beside Gracie's mother, Becky. She clung to her baby's lifeless body, purple in her trembling arms.

Hour turned to hour as I listened, loved, and prayed, offering nothing but my presence.

A nurse came in to bathe Gracie and make a keepsake cast from her tiny hands and feet. When I escaped for a bit to the chapel, I unleashed my pent-up grief.

*God, I'm in over my head. I don't understand this. I need you to give me the words to lead them through these next pivotal minutes. Please—don't let me be trite. I don't want to say the wrong thing. Help me hold it together for them.*

When I returned to the room, I found more grieving relatives had joined them, including Gracie's father's pastor and Gracie's grandfather, who was also a pastor. What was I doing here with all these pastors who the family knew so much better? How had I come to be invited to such a painful, precious moment?

Gracie wore a frilly pink dress in her mama's arms. I set my hand on Becky's shoulder and unleashed a passionate prayer that could have only come from the secret place. A place brimming with comfort, truth, and strength.

Peace hovered in the room when I opened my teary eyes. Gracie's grandfather, the pastor, leaned toward me. "*That* was one of the most powerful prayers I've ever heard."

"Thank you, Jesus," I whispered.

A knock rattled the door, and in stepped the nurse from the morgue, who had come to receive Gracie. "Are you ready, dear?"

Becky finally released her baby. "Goodbye, honey. We'll always love you."

Tears fell in a holy hush.

*Thank you, God, for helping me stand with a family in their most sacred space. Now if you could please help me out on the home front.*

7

# Marriage Meltdown

"When will things get better than same?
Why is it so cold again and again?"

– Josiah Cullen

**Summer 2011**

"I miss my wife," Joe told me one night.

Our marriage had hit an iceberg, and cold water seeped through the cracks. After work each day, I stepped into a forest of Josiah's endless needs. He'd get me up in the night, and then I'd have to down a twenty-four-ounce cup of gas station coffee before sprinting off to lead my team.

Joe and I had always known my work responsibilities would add a burden to him, but what could I do? We'd agreed on this arrangement, and now I had commitments to keep. Besides, what would it hurt Joe to spend extra time with our son?

But Joe had hit a spiritual dry patch. In fact, the closer I grew to God, the more he seemed to run in the other direction. I'd ask him if we could pray together for wisdom about certain things, like whether or not we should try the Rapid Prompting Method, and he'd respond with frustration.

"What's the point?" he said. "Whenever I ask God for something, he does the opposite."

What had happened to the man who wouldn't miss a single

night in his read-through-the-Bible plan? The man who used to memorize a Scripture verse a week?

When he found the highlighted book of Bible promises I'd left in the bathroom, he held it in front of me. "What's this?"

I swallowed. "Just something I hoped you might read."

"You think you have this all figured out, don't you?"

"Not really. I just want to help."

"Well, I'm not like you, Tahni."

What was happening? Was this his situational depression acting up? Either way, the growing rift between us threatened to swallow me whole. How could two people with backgrounds and jobs in communication not be able to talk to each other when we used to carry on for hours?

As newlyweds we used to say, "What's the big deal about the first years of marriage? They're easy." Ever since Josiah's autism diagnosis, though, we had gone backward. We hit bump after bump on a long, winding road that only left us in a ditch like so many other autism families: banged up, flat, and tired.

One evening as we lay in bed, everything came to a head.

"It's been a busy week," I said. "And now I have to teach membership class on Thursday, because Heath can't make it."

Joe pressed his lips together. "This Thursday? Ah, that's not going to work. Judy needs me to run the camera at the commission meeting."

"Uh, can't they get someone else? I'm the only person who's been trained to teach this class, and a hundred people are depending on it."

"Sorry, Tahni, but I need to do this. I haven't been helping with the extra things like other people do. I told Judy she could count on me."

"Well, I need to count on you too. It's hard for me to find someone else to teach a membership class. They've trained me specifically for this purpose, and I *need* to teach this class. I'm sure you're not the only person who can stand behind a camera."

Joe sat up. "Why am I always the one to sacrifice everything? You act like your career and everything you do at the church is more important than what I do. My stuff is important too, you know."

"I know it is, Joe, but you have to look at this logically. It would be a whole lot easier for them to replace you than for the people at church to replace me, given the circumstances. Since someone needs to be home with Josiah, logically, that would be you."

He crossed his arms. "I've lost my wife to another man, and I can't do a single thing about it—because it's God. God is the man who has taken you away from me!"

Heat rose to my face as I sat up. "You couldn't have said anything more hurtful. If it wasn't for God, I wouldn't even be able to breathe. Well, at least God loves me!"

He jumped out of bed. "Listen to you. You're talking nonsense. I can't take it anymore. You've ruined my life! If I hadn't met you, I'd probably be a network TV anchor on a major station in North Dakota. But no, you had to go and move us all the way out here. You make all these big decisions and then I just have to go with it. Well, you know what? My life sucks."

I glared at him. "Well, if your life sucks, it isn't my fault. If it weren't for me, we'd never get anywhere in making decisions. People grow up, you know. They have to make decisions about buying houses, having a family, and even looking for a new job if they want one. But no, you're the king of mediocrity!"

"Thanks a lot!" he said. "Sure, wait until now to tell me how you really feel about me. Well, I hate it here!"

"Fine. Then maybe we should part ways. I'll take Josiah with me. I'll start over and live near my mom if I have to. You can go back to North Dakota and live in your parents' basement for all I care! That way, I can take all this responsibility off your poor little shoulders, and you won't even have to worry about a thing except for yourself."

I stormed out, slamming the door. Then I jumped in the car

and drove off crying. He'd worry about me, and it would serve him right. I stopped at a nearby park and turned off my lights, bawling and blubbering—until someone knocked on my window.

"Everything okay in there, ma'am?"

I gasped, wiping my eyes. "Officer! Oh, hi. Yeah, nothing major. Just one of those nights. You know, the kind when you want to be alone and have a good cry? Uh—is there a problem with me being parked here? I figured it would be better than cruising around like a mad woman. Know what I mean?"

He sniffed a laugh. "Go ahead and take your time. Have a good night."

When I returned home close to midnight, I found Joe staring at the ceiling. I could tell from his breathing that he'd been crying.

"I'm sorry," I said, grabbing his hand.

"Me too."

"Are we going to make it, Joe?"

"Yes. We're both just stressed and tired."

I cleared my throat. "Um, I think this will take a bigger fix than sleep and rest. Joe, I'm really mad at you, but I love you. So goodnight."

We did ourselves a favor and went to a counselor. One with wild floppy hair and a collection of *Lord of the Rings* statues, who just listened to us go back and forth.

"I wonder if he's ever going to say anything," I told Joe in the car. "Or will we just keep doing all the talking ourselves? Because if he doesn't ever talk to us, we might as well give the one hundred dollars to a homeless man. Toss some money into his can and complain all we want in front of him."

On our tenth session, the counselor shoved his notepad aside. "We're going to give you each some crayons and a TV tray. I counsel kids as well as adults, and one of the ways they like to express themselves is by drawing pictures. I thought it might be fun for each of you to personify the most difficult emotion that keeps triggering you. Draw that monster emotion and give him a name."

Joe and I couldn't help ourselves. We laughed. Was this guy for real? The last time I'd drawn a picture was at the conference in Redding, and believe me, this was no treasure hunt. Fine, I'd do it. I grabbed a red crayon and drew a big, puffy, messed-up-looking dust ball.

"Who do we have here?" asked the counselor.

"I think I'll name him Push, because that's what I feel like."

Then Joe showed his sketch of a small, wiry green monster. "Say hello to Clive."

"Good, good," the counselor said. "Keep it up, guys. Tahni, tell me about Push."

"Push never lets me get any rest. There's always someone else I need to take care of. Some other job that needs to be done. The minute I sit down—bam—someone else needs a piece of me. As soon as I get one storm under control, Push stirs up the dust."

"Great, great. Go on."

"I just want someone to step in and take care of the things that keep getting pushed at Push. Then maybe I wouldn't feel so responsible for dealing with everything and feeling like a failure if I didn't."

"Beautiful," he said. "Joe, tell me about Clive."

Joe stared off, looking nothing like the television producer whose deep-canyon voice echoed across the airwaves. "Clive makes me feel small and scared. I want to be strong and confident, but Clive tells me I'm a fraud and no one cares what I think. Clive mocks me for not being handy enough and for not knowing how to fix problems in my family. If I can't fix a toilet, how can I fix the big stuff? Clive tells me I'm not as important as other people and that it wouldn't even matter if I wasn't here."

"Aha!" the counselor said. "We're finally getting somewhere.

Tahni, I want you to imagine pulling Push out of yourself." He gave a dramatic tug on his shirt as if pulling him out. "Joe, I want you to pull out Clive. Push and Clive represent your insecurities that keep fighting and jabbing each other. The real you doesn't want to hurt the other because you care. But Push and Clive keep getting in the way and making a lot of extra noise in your heads."

"But Joe makes me feel so bad about myself."

"No. Joe can never *make* you feel anything about yourself. You're in charge of how you feel."

Thanks to our sessions, Joe and I began to open up in healthier ways. We even started having date nights.

One night, as we sat in the car, I told him, "I'm reading a book called *You Don't Have to Be Wrong to Repent.*"

"Good title," he said. "I'll definitely keep that in mind during our next argument."

"Very funny," I said, rolling my eyes. "Like you're the one who's always right."

He grinned. "I knew you'd like that one, babe."

As Joe's eyes twinkled, I was reminded of the healing power of laughter. It had always been a faithful companion in our marriage. Clearly God knew what he was doing.

*Thank you, Lord. With you in control, I'm sure things will only get better from here.*

## 8

# Rapid Prompting

"I'm not lost in this place of my thinking.
I'm lost in my performing like all are."

– Josiah Cullen

*July 2011*

Ever since seeing *A Mother's Courage*, I couldn't stop thinking about the Rapid Prompting Method. Through an online search, I discovered that its amazing founder, Soma, had actually started an RPM training center in Austin, Texas. Also, Erika Anderson, a former applied behavioral analysis (ABA) therapist who apprenticed under Soma, offered a four-day "summer camp" program in Green Bay, Wisconsin.

Either this method would work or it wouldn't. I found the online videos quite convincing—but hadn't I thought the same thing about the hyperbaric oxygen chamber? Why would I want to venture out on another pricey limb? I didn't. But I also didn't want to miss out on something that might help our boy communicate.

"Hi, Erika," I said into the phone. "I'm interested in your camps. Do you take children as young as five?"

"Oh, I love the little ones," she said. "They have a shorter attention span, but they often excel with RPM."

"How much is the four-day session?"

"Around five hundred dollars. We still have openings, but they're filling fast."

"Well, I'm interested."

Hanging up, my heart swelled with hope. It wouldn't be cheap with the hotel and travel costs, but it just might be worth it.

Joe gave me his blessing and the church gave me the time off. Everything seemed to fit into place for me and our five-year-old to check out this unusual communication method. I packed our clothes and toys and went to bed extra early to prepare for my five-hour drive.

At two o'clock in the morning, a strange watery feeling crept in my gut. No … I barely made it to the bathroom before throwing up. Food poisoning? Flu? Nerves? I couldn't tell, but whatever it was, it had to go!

*Get behind me, Satan! Josiah and I are doing this thing, in Jesus' name! Father, you're going to have to heal me.*

I hugged the toilet for the rest of the night, but my stomach only grew worse.

*We're still going*, I told myself right up until it was time to leave. Buckling Josiah in the back, I popped prayers like Pepto-Bismols, trying to ignore the worry slamming my brain.

*What if I throw up in the car and have to keep stopping on the highway? What if I couldn't learn fast enough and turned out to be a lousy teacher?*

*Stop*, I told myself. The flood of what-ifs wouldn't exactly help my sour stomach and sleep-deprived brain.

Everything went well for the first hour. Josiah quietly entertained himself with puzzles on the iPad. But then he cranked down the window and air shot through my ears, igniting my headache.

"Josiah, I thought you were over that phase. Roll it up!" If he understood me at all, he didn't act like it. I had to pull over and crank it up myself. "Don't touch it again!"

Ten minutes later, he rolled it back down, and *voom* went my patience.

"Josiah, I am *not* going to play this game. Keep the window up! Hey, why don't you play with your musical toys? We'll soon be at a McDonald's, and I'll buy you a burger."

Ten minutes passed, and he rolled it down again. This time, he chucked out his remote control toy. *Great,* I thought, watching through the mirror as it shattered to pieces on the highway. *Now all I need is to have a cop pull me over for littering.* He'd probably tell me to get a grip on my son. And I'd say, "Wish I could, sir. My son might look like a typical five-year-old, but he has a whole different set of wiring."

When we arrived at the hotel that evening, I parked, lugged in our stuff, and grabbed Josiah's hand. But the instant we entered our room, the kid got all revved up and ready to fly. He jumped on the king-sized bed, leaped off a chair, and bounded back to the bed.

"Joe…" I groaned into the phone. "I think this was a bad idea. Josiah is going to wake up the whole hotel. How can we survive four nights of this and hold it together for therapy?"

Morning held new hope when we stepped into a room with Erika. She gave new meaning to the phrase "rapid prompting." Therapists typically spend a couple weeks getting to know a child before jumping into lessons, but with just four days here, we had to get right to business.

The small white room didn't have any pictures or frills, just a basic desk with chairs, to minimize distractions. Josiah lunged for the blinds and managed to get tangled up in the strings.

"No Josiah!" I shouted, pulling him out. "Ugh. Sorry about that."

"No problem. Josiah, we're going to have fun today. Come have a seat by the wall." She moved to his right and hemmed him between the wall and the desk so he'd feel more protected.

As she spoke to Josiah, he became silly and wiggly and made

loud noises. He stared at the shadows on the blinds, then hyper-focused on the lights, which Erika promptly turned off.

"Josiah, would you like to talk about famous people or animals?" As Erika presented the two options, she wrote them on a piece of paper, tore it down the middle, and placed each piece about six inches apart in front of him.

"Famous people?" she asked, slapping the paper, "or animals?" *Slap.* "You choose."

Without missing a beat, Josiah slapped the paper that said *famous people*, then handed it to her.

"Good. Now I'm going to talk to you about the man who discovered our country, but first I want to ask you a question. Do we live in America or Europe? You choose."

What? I was still in shock that he'd picked *famous people*. But now he picked *America*? I could hardly restrain my excitement.

Erika reached for a book, *What Every Kindergartner Needs to Know*. No stinking way. Josiah wasn't even halfway close to kindergarten topics, but Erika flipped it open and removed a short lesson plan.

"You're right. We live in America. People from many different nations live in America, but it wasn't always that way. In fact, I want to talk to you about a man named Christopher Columbus." She wrote down Christopher's name so Josiah could see it. As usual, his eyes looked elsewhere, but she kept going.

"Christopher Columbus was an explorer from Spain, and he sailed the ocean blue in 1492 in a ship." She ripped the paper in half. "What did Christopher sail in? Did he sail in a S-H-I-P ship"—*slap*—"or in a C-A-R car?" *Slap.*

My breath caught in my throat as Josiah smacked the word *ship*. Either this was a fluke or he really knew the answer.

"That's right, Josiah. Christopher Columbus did sail in a ship. He gathered a whole crew of people and set out in three ships. The ships were named *Nina*, *Pinta*, and *Santa Maria*."

I teared up as Erika read the rest of the story. I couldn't believe it. My son was being taught meaningful things, and he understood what she was saying. This wasn't just a matter of "touch the red square" or "where is the letter A?" This woman had unlocked my son and shown me that he was actually in there!

I sat stunned as she shared from a patchwork of subjects like history, telling time, and photosynthesis. She did tricks with voice variation, adding emphasis on keywords. Then she used her finger to draw on his hand. She had him touch rough objects like Scotch-tape to distract his senses.

Josiah kept hopping out of his chair, wiggling, and giggling, but Erika refused to let it bother her. She simply pulled him back to the lesson and kept going. Josiah missed some of the answers involving choices, but he answered 80 percent of the questions correctly! So much for all the negative things people said about his receptive language being impaired.

In the afternoon session, Erika had already turned off the lights and tucked back the blind strings. Josiah went right to his chair, appearing somewhat amiable.

"We're going to do math," Erika said.

Had I heard her correctly? Josiah didn't know the first thing about math. Not even two plus one. But she counted from one to ten, slapping the beats on the table. Then she did the whole rip-and-write routine. "What number comes after seven? Is it four"—*slap*—"or eight?" *Slap.* "You choose."

His hand crashed down on number eight.

"Good. Let's do it again. If you have eight pencils and you take away one, how many do you have left? Three"—*slam*—"or seven?" *Slam.* "You choose."

*Bam.* His hand went down on number seven. Was I seeing things, or did his face actually glow with fresh pride? Well, I was proud of him too. And after this, I'd never be able to look at him the same.

"You can tell a lot from his unique sounds and movements,"

Erika told me. "His stims are a natural way to show his learning channel. Josiah's an auditory listener."

"He is?"

"Yes, and that's why you need to talk to him as if you're talking to a child who's blind. Talk to him all the time. Tell him what you see all around you because that will help him learn new things. Read to him. I don't mean toddler books. Read him books appropriate for kids his own age. Remember this: assume age-level intelligence."

Wow. Talk about a perspective shift. Since Josiah didn't talk, my conversations with him usually defaulted to either short phrases or silence. I mean, what mom wants to talk to a wall or have her words land in a big puddle of nothingness?

Now that I'd been handed the golden key, that would all change. Erika gave me permission to launch into something I'd always loved: education. Lessons that went beyond labeling and flash card drills to the new world of solid, useful, expand-your-mind communication.

I returned to the hotel on a high, but it didn't last very long because Josiah wouldn't stop bouncing off the walls. By three thirty in the morning, I'd had enough.

"We're out of here," I said, rushing us outside. I had to go somewhere, anywhere but crazy.

It took twenty minutes of driving around before Josiah finally slumped to the side. Now I just had to find a parking lot to catch some sleep myself.

*Okay, God. I see a church. It looks great—so long as a cop doesn't come knocking on my window again.*

Our last session ended with thank-yous, encouragement, and bittersweet goodbyes. "You know what time it is, JoJo?" I said, buckling him in the car. "It's time for Culvers."

We sat down as soon as we arrived. I grabbed a paper, tore it in half, and wrote out a couple words for our menu.

"Josiah, what kind of food would you like? A hamburger"—
*slap*—"or chicken nuggets?" *Slap*.

He slapped *hamburger*, and I couldn't believe how the whole
world had opened up. RPM didn't just empower me, it also gave
my son a voice. I wouldn't need to thrust everything on him. He
would now have his own options and opinions.

After we finished, we drove to a park. A pale silver moon hung
in the cool July night. Josiah ran for the swings, and I grabbed the
one beside him, eager to unleash the dam that had been locked
up tight all these years. "JoJo, look at the tree. Did you know God
made each leaf with its own tiny set of veins? Summer will soon
end, and we'll start a brand-new season. These leaves will turn
pretty colors and fall from the branches. Just look at these trees.
Birch, maple, oak. They all add their own unique share of beauty
to the world.

"Did you know this park is near Lambeau Field where the
Packers play? Football is the most popular American sport, and
people watch it from all over the world."

I wanted to shout, "Goodbye, old routines!" I'd found my son!
After all these years, God had made a way for me to get to know
him. I hopped off my swing and gave him a squeeze as a breeze
blew through my hair. "I'm proud of you, Josiah."

I cocked my head to the side. The moon appeared brighter now,
and the sliver almost looked like a smile. Amazing how perspective
changes everything. Mine had flipped in a heartbeat, and it picked
up even more as I thought of all the new books I could use to teach
Josiah about life.

*God, I can learn the inner workings of my boy. Thanks for helping
me dream again.*

A short while later, I had a strange dream about attending the
grand opening of a prestigious art gallery in uptown Minneapolis.

*What should I wear?* I wondered. Blue jeans wouldn't cut it, so
in my dream I rummaged through my closet until I found just the

thing: a crisp, nicely ironed white shirt. Then I pulled out a navy skirt and a snazzy pair of heels to go with it.

I had a vague idea of what to expect at an art gallery. Paintings would be evenly spaced on white walls. Sculptures would be displayed on pristine platforms, and people would walk around with furrowed brows, scratching their chins while scrutinizing art.

I turned the knob of the solid white door, excited to dip into culture. The instant I stepped in, my senses went into overdrive. I'd entered a booming raucous party. People moved freely, laughing, joking. Strangely, the larger-than-life paintings overlapped each other, tilting at odd angles.

Forget bow-tied attendants passing tiny hors d'oeuvres with toothpicks. Instead, people passed heaping bowls of couscous or some kind of Middle Eastern dish topped with nuts, dates, and apricots. And everybody dipped in, helping themselves.

In front of the fireplace mantel stood the sculpture of all sculptures. Bursting with color, the bamboo piece arose from the foundation with its green curly parts corkscrewing all the way to the ceiling.

A flash of movement caught my eye from the left. That's when I turned and saw a gorgeous blond-haired woman reclining on a bright red velvet lounge. Her long curly hair cascaded to the side, covering the floral pattern on her loose-fitting Bohemian-style gown.

She gazed at me intently, then extended her arm with its flared-out sleeve and pointed at the bamboo sculpture.

"Tahni." She said my name with calm confidence and authority. "God, the creator of the universe, does not create in straight lines."

I woke up in a daze, slammed with questions. *Crazy dream! What in the world could it possibly mean?*

## 9

# Out of This World

"The results of trusting God are too true to be bad."
– Josiah Cullen

*October 2011*

I opened my supply box and placed our RPM goodies on the kitchen table: a ream of white copy paper, a handful of number two pencils, the alphabet stencil boards, a visual timer, and of course, a stack of user-friendly learning books.

"Come on, Josiah. Let's get started." I led him to his chair and cracked open a fruit book, rich in colors and shapes. I flipped to the banana page I'd prepared in advance for our lesson, but Josiah, bless his dear little annoying heart, leaped off his chair and ran to his room.

"Oh no you don't, kiddo!" I grabbed him under his arms and walked him right back to the table. "If we're going to learn, you need to stay." I cleared my throat. "Bananas grow in clusters. They start green, and when they turn yellow they are ready to eat."

He slunk like a jellyfish and landed on the floor near Lucy, our Maltipoo.

"Hey, I need you back in your chair." Readjusting him, I pressed his shoulder to keep him there. *Woo-hoo.* I read a few more sentences, but when I removed my pressing-down hand to grab a piece of paper, he hightailed it to the living room and began jumping on the couch, laughing.

"Josiah, we're going to get you back in that chair, and you are going to stay there as long as it takes for us to actually get somewhere." His body sagged as I carried him to the kitchen in a battle I had to win.

"People eat more bananas than apples and oranges combined."

He squealed, then jumped to his feet and lunged for the refrigerator.

"Stop!" But it was too late. He'd already jammed his arms in and knocked over the ketchup and salad dressing.

*Keep going*, I told myself. *You know he has it in him to learn.*

"Okay, let's try math. Mama bear gave birth to five cubs and two ran away. How many baby bears does mama have left? One bear or three bears? You choose." I handed him a pencil so he could poke the right number in the stencil, and I waited for three seconds. *Slam.* The pencil went to the floor.

Okay, what would Erika do? She'd hand him another pencil, so that's what I did. *Wham.* It joined its buddy on the floor. Then Josiah crumbled right down to join them too.

*Anne Sullivan, how did you do it?* I'd always respected the woman who had trained deaf, mute, and blind Helen Keller. While others treated the extremely difficult Helen like a helpless, hopeless castaway, Anne, known for her grit, compassion, and perseverance, always believed in Helen's teachableness.

Ironically, in his senior year of college, Joe had been cast as Helen Keller's father for their big production. The two of us had stayed up late watching the old black-and-white version of *The Miracle Worker.* Who would have ever thought it would come to this?

My twenty-five-minute session with Josiah morphed into a lesson about how to sit and stay in the chair—without going bananas.

"Is this normal?" I asked Erika on the phone. "Do other students give their parents such a rough time?"

"Yes," she assured me. "But I can give you a few helpful tips if you'd like. For starters, make your voice more interesting than your surroundings. You'll also want to vary your tone and speed. Go from quiet, to joyful, to playful, to over-the-top. Can you do that?"

"What, this drama girl?" I said. "Why, of course."

I watched an online video of a mother using RPM to teach her son while chasing him all over the house. That mom refused to let her boy's inability to calm down prevent her from teaching and communicating.

Fine. If she could put on her workout shoes, so could I.

"Hey, wait up!" My voice trailed after Josiah as he zoomed to his room carrying my stencils and pencils. Catching up to him, I discovered the woman was right. The more I loosened up, the more Josiah and I could connect.

I pressed in for several months, but didn't get very far. I began to wonder if I should try some of the same principles on Josiah's iPad. Maybe if he learned to press large letters, he would see the fruit of his thoughts and feel more involved with the creative process. At least it couldn't hurt to try.

"Here's what the word M-O-M looks like," I said, speaking it out as I typed. "Okay, now it's your turn. I'll say the letter, then you can press it."

To give Josiah comfort and ground him like a helium balloon on a string, I did what I saw other helpers do. I gently supported his arm and waited for his finger to find the first letter.

He touched the M, but then he ran off.

Ugh! It had been a whole year since Green Bay, and I felt like a tire stuck in a snow bank. Every time my six-year-old rocketed away like this, he took along with him my dreams of ever teaching him to read or write.

One morning, as I sat praying in Caribou Coffee, my cell phone rang.

"Is this Tahni?" asked a woman with something like a Russian accent.

"Yes, it is," I said, trying to figure out who this was.

"My name is Cynthia. I hope you don't mind, but Erika gave me your number. I have a daughter with autism, and we've been learning RPM. We've kind of hit a bump in the road and could really use a refresher class. Erika agreed to come to the Cities for three days if I could find a couple of families to join me. Do you think this is something you'd be interested in?"

"Yes," I said quickly.

"Fabulous. I own a realty company. We could meet at my office."

So that's what we did a few Saturdays later. Cynthia led Joe, Josiah, and me into a conference room where we dropped off Josiah, then stepped into an office across the hall.

Erika explained we could watch one-on-one sessions on closed-circuit TV. Also, to help us parents maximize our learning time, we could watch each other's kids as well.

"This is Joe's first time to see this in person," I told the ladies. "Joe, I can't wait for you to see how Erika works with him."

Erika scooted close to Josiah and pulled out a book. Seconds later, Josiah jumped off his chair and did a headstand. I slapped my forehead and groaned.

"That's okay." One of the ladies patted my shoulder. "We get it."

"Hey there, smart boy," Erika said without a hint of stress. "Let's watch you walk back to your chair like this." She ducked, bobbed, and maneuvered like a wrestler, while defending herself from Josiah's flailing arms.

Josiah plopped back in the chair, and Erika began her questions. "What do you want to learn? Math, English, or something else?"

Three options? I felt my eyes bug out. He could hardly handle two.

She wrote each one out, and I held my breath as Josiah pointed to math.

"Good choice," she said. "Let's spell math." She grabbed the right stencil board and stuck a pencil in his hand. Joe and I stared in utter amazement as the pencil went in the air and poked down on the letter M.

"Great. Now stay focused."

He did as she asked, and poked the letter A.

"Terrific. Keep going."

He poked the T.

"That's right. Almost there."

He went for H!

Joe laughed, shaking his head, and I turned to the ladies. "I've always had to tell him each letter, one at a time."

"You have one car," Erika said. "What color do you want the car to be? Is it between A–I, J–R, or S–Z?" She wrote each option on a paper, tore it in three pieces, and tapped as she said it. "You choose."

The point of his pencil came down on *A–I* and a smile lit his face.

"Okay, what's the first letter?" Erika held up the A-I stencil.

His pencil poked through the B.

She rewrote the stencil options for Josiah's next letter, and he chose J–R.

"Good. What letter would you like?"

He hopped out of his chair and flapped his arms.

"Josiah, let's see what color this car will be. First we have it starting with a B. Now we have from J–R. What letter do you pick?"

His pencil came down on the R.

Joe and I looked at each other, mouths wide open, as he spelled B-R-O-W-N.

"Did you see that, Joe? He didn't just spell a small three-letter word he might have seen at school. Oh my gosh. If he'd spelled blue, it would have been amazing enough—but he spelled a five-letter word all by himself."

The ladies clapped and cheered.

When the session came to a close, I shook Erika's hand. "I can't thank you enough. I feel like you've renewed our hope. At home we've been experimenting with the letter board app on an iPad."

"Oh, I don't recommend that," she said. "It's important to keep things in order. RPM works best if you move from stencils to a circular laminated letter board, and then maybe to a laminated paper letter board. Motor planning and mastering each step of independent pointing is just as important as content. I'd encourage you to try all those phases before you venture into anything electronic."

Too late. Sometimes Josiah communicated by poking his pencil on the alphabet stencil holes. But lately he'd tried pointing to letters on the iPad. Since he actually preferred it, we kept using it. I didn't want to backtrack.

For our next lesson at home, I grabbed some of Josiah's favorite Froggy books and worked on a song I'd turned into a game with hand motions.

"Head it, boot it, knee it, shoot it—but don't use your hands."

We played the game so many times that Josiah began to memorize the words. If I left one out, which I'd do intentionally, he'd know exactly how to spell it on the iPad. Hurray! I'd finally figured out how to give him options while cranking up the fun factor.

On September 15, 2012, six weeks after our refresher class, and just a little less than one month before Josiah turned seven, we sat at the table for another home lesson.

"JoJo, would you like to work from your *Everybody Poops* book or from your Children's Bible? Poop or Bible? You choose."

His hand came down on the word *Bible*, so I reached for the Children's Bible with one hand and grabbed the materials with the other.

Josiah lunged for the couch and burst into giggles.

"Hey, get back to the dining table. We need to finish." I might as well have shouted to the wind. He snuck in another bounce before I could pull him to his feet.

"Stay!" I sat him in front of the timer and pinned his leg. For all my jumping up to juggle papers, pencils, and stencils, it's no wonder why I felt like an octopus with revolving arms.

Josiah breathed in and out like a racehorse. I had to act fast.

"Listen close, okay?" I tapped the book. "Jesus spit on the ground and made mud. He placed the mud on the blind man's eyes. The blind man did what Jesus said, and then he could see."

I snatched a sheet of paper, ripped it down the middle, wrote out his two choices, and placed the halves in front of him. "Focus, Josiah. Jesus healed the blind man. What did he do? Did Jesus H-E-A-L heal the blind man or did he P-L-A-Y play with the blind man? Heal or play? You choose."

With a fiery jerk of his body, he poked his pencil to the first one, *heal*.

"Good!" I picked up his iPad and scooted closer. Steadying his forearm, a limb with a mind of its own, I let my closeness comfort his oversaturated sensory world. My light touch on his arm grounded him as I loosely dangled his arm over the large alphabet keys. "Time to spell."

"Ahh," he groaned as his index finger circled the air and came in for a landing. Whoops. He hit the G instead of the H.

"Focus, Josiah."

But his finger went for the O. What was he writing? GO? More jabs at the screen, and he spelled out something entirely different:

**godisagoodgiftgiver**

My brain hiccupped as I leaned close. Even without spaces, the message rang clear. God is a good gift giver. I gasped. He'd only ever spelled a few simple words, but now, right before my eyes, he'd written his first independent sentence.

"H-how did you do that?"

His finger returned to the touchscreen.

**God is everlasting Jehovah.**

My mind tripped as the room spun. Josiah had *never* been taught such a thing. *God is everlasting Jehovah?* Joe and I didn't even talk like that—so formal and reverent. Keep breathing. He must have picked it up from somewhere. But from where? Who taught him how to spell like this, in full sentences spilling theological truth?

"Josiah, how do you know this?"

His finger dropped to the screen, and with a shaky voice, I spoke the letters as he typed them. "A … U …" What now? Was he trying to spell *autism?*

Wait. No. It couldn't be. He'd typed the word *Auntie.* My hand flew over my mouth, and I felt the color drain from my face as he typed the next words.

**Auntie told an angel to tell me.**

I could barely swallow. I had never breathed a word to him about Auntie. Shaking, the memories and guilt came flooding back. I handed Josiah a musical toy and slowly backed away to call my mom.

"Something strange just happened to Josiah." I laughed and cried at the same time.

"Tell me, what's going on?"

I blubbered out what had happened, and she burst with excitement. "Praise you, Jesus! Tahni, this is awesome. What a mighty God we serve!"

Joe was out of town for a work conference, and when I called him that evening he sounded bewildered and overjoyed at the same time. "That's incredible, babe. Wish I was there."

"I know," I said. "This is huge. Our son must have had some kind of spiritual encounter. God must be healing him!"

"Crazy. I can't wait to hear more about it."

Well, that made two of us. I hurried to Josiah's room to ask more questions.

# 10

# Major Discoveries

"I am not listening to lies, I am kissing the skies."
– Josiah Cullen

*September 2012*

Scooting beside Josiah's small-framed body, I crawled under the covers with him. "Before you fall asleep, JoJo, I have a question for you. I was wondering ... did the angel say anything else?" I squeezed the iPad and watched in amazement as the screen came to life.

**Auntie hugs of gladness. God is good all the time. Hugs of delight. God of wonder. God is very capable.**

Tears filled my eyes. "Yes, sweetie. He *is* very capable." *Keep it steady*, I told myself, rising to my feet. "Okay, it's time to say goodnight. Sweet dreams."

I rested the heavy blanket on his jumpy legs. Then, as if life was normal, I planted a kiss on the middle of his cheek and started the MeMoves app on his iPad. Hopefully, the calming music and visual movements would help him relax and fall asleep. I knew it would take more than that for me though.

Collapsing on my bed, I stared at the ceiling. *What's going on, God? You wouldn't mess with me, would you? How is it possible for Auntie to talk to an angel? And how could my son have an angelic visitation?*

I grabbed my Bible from the end table and turned to Hebrews. "These were all commended for their faith, yet none of them received what had been promised, since God had planned something better for us so that only together with us would they be made perfect. Therefore, since we are surrounded by such a great cloud of witnesses, let us throw off everything that hinders and the sin that so easily entangles" (Hebrews 11:39–12:1).

I had always known the cloud of witnesses referred to the Old Testament saints—but did they also refer to our own family members? Could they be cheering us on every day? If that was the case, Auntie loved Jesus, so she'd certainly be among them.

Good old Auntie. Grandma had inherited her sister who never married. After my mom grew up, she inherited Auntie, but technically, I inherited Auntie more than any of them. I was the one who had to share my room with her for the bulk of my adolescent years.

Each night Auntie would slip into her boyish pajamas with their button-down pants. Then she'd grab her shiny green can of Bag Balm, the stuff they used to rub on cow udders. She'd prop up her legs and slather the soles of her feet until she smelled like a combination of herbs, petroleum jelly, and eucalyptus oil.

Auntie kept active in her small world of geranium gardens, but she didn't have any friends outside of our family, and she never learned to drive. Strangely, she had a consuming fear of cars going out of gear. Nobody could quite figure it out, but we all knew.

After Auntie fixed her feet, she'd perch her glasses on the tip of her nose and hold her book a few inches away. When I was ten, she read to me the entire Little House on the Prairie series. I liked her historical commentary the best. "Oh, that dear girl Laura," she said. "I feel like I practically grew up with her."

Auntie took more interest in me than in my older brothers, which meant she also had higher expectations. "How did you do on your math test?" she asked when I came home from school one day.

I beamed proudly as I handed her my congratulations slip with an A- I'd worked especially hard for.

"Oh, honey," she said, clicking her tongue and shaking her head. "I'm sure you'll do better next time."

All these years later, that memory suddenly sprang to life with a fresh realization. Throughout Josiah's steady stream of tests and evaluations, I'd always felt I couldn't measure up or do enough. That's why I kept trying harder. Could my endless grasping be connected to the seeds of insecurity planted so many years ago?

Another memory resurfaced and took me back to when I was fifteen. Our family had just moved back to my parents' tiny hometown of Timber Lake, South Dakota.

My mom always said, "You've got to take what you have and do something with it." With little money to her name, she started a small gift shop in Grandpa and Grandma's old fixer-upper.

As much as I appreciated Mom's motto about making the best of things, I couldn't do that myself—at least not when it came to Auntie. That eighty-nine-year-old lady got on my nerves worse than a flea on a puppy.

Ever since leaving my old friends in Phoenix, I had questions about school life that only a mom could answer. I'd been trying to catch her alone, but with Auntie around, it felt nearly impossible.

One night, however, I heard Mom holler in the kitchen. "Oh no!" I hurried over. "What is it?"

"I forgot to unplug the potpourri pot," she said. "I need to go back to the store and take care of it. Tahni, would you like to come with me?"

My heart soared. "Yes, I'd love to." At last, the perfect opportunity.

That's when I heard a voice from around the corner. "I'll go with you too." Oh no. Auntie.

Heat rose to my face as I folded my arms firmly in front of my chest. "Well, if she's going, then I'm not!" I threw an angry look at Auntie, stormed to my room—to our room—and cranked up the music. How dare she interrupt my mom time again?

"I hate you!" I screamed into the empty house.

Twenty-five minutes later, I got a phone call from Vera, my mom's longtime friend, who also happened to be the sheriff's wife. Vera lived across the street from Mom's shop. From the moment she spoke my name, I could tell something was wrong.

"There's been an accident. I'll tell you the details when we get there."

Vera, Mom, and I followed the ambulance to the nearest hospital forty miles away, and I listened in stunned silence as they unpacked the story.

Mom had kept the truck running, and Auntie stayed in it while Mom ran in to deal with the potpourri. Not a big deal, but of all the crazy improbabilities—the truck went out of gear.

Panicking, Auntie jumped out to the driveway as the truck started moving. Since she had left her door open, it knocked her over, and the front tire pinned the edge of her hip.

My Aunt Jane, who met us at the hospital, stood beside me at Auntie's bedside while the nurse talked to us. "She doesn't have any broken bones, but she went into shock. She seems stable enough though."

"Thank God," said Aunt Jane, "because she looks like she's been through the war."

"Auntie?" I said weakly. "Auntie? It's good to see you again."

Her eyes fluttered as she tried to speak, but I couldn't make out the muffled words. Frustrated but determined to make amends later, I dragged myself to the waiting room and sat with Mom as she filled out the paperwork.

Less than three minutes later, they called a code. Doctors and nurses rushed to Auntie's room with a cart. Her heart had stopped.

I shot Mom a helpless look. "Aren't they going to try to restart it?"

Sadness darkened her face as she shook her head. "Auntie wrote in her wishes, 'Do not resuscitate.' Her heart couldn't take it. I'm sorry, sweetie."

Tsunami-sized guilt rolled over me. Guilt that had stuck in my heart all these years and refused to let go. Guilt that had pushed Auntie's name far away from my mind and lips—until now.

Thoughts about Josiah and Auntie rose and fell like waves until I fell asleep exhausted. Then, at three in the morning, Josiah ran into my room, over-stimulated.

"What's up, buddy?" I flipped on our lamp and grabbed the iPad.

**Hope**, he wrote.

"Hope for what?" I asked.

**Hope for autism. Save me.**

Would someone pinch me and say this was a dream? "Okay, Josiah, what are you talking about? Tell me what you mean by *save me*."

He bounded toward the living room, and I followed him to the couch. "By any chance, did that angel tell you his name?"

**Raphael. God gave men and women and children good news. No more sickness and pain.**

My heart pounded. I had only heard of two Raphaels, the Teenage Mutant Ninja Turtle and the famous Italian painter.

As Josiah bounced, I googled and quickly found an article about the angel Raphael. Interestingly, the article said the Catholic Bible mentioned him in a wisdom book called Tobit. Great. I could see it now: my Protestant friends would find out about this and think I was a heretic.

The article described Raphael as an angel who protects, and his name meant "God heals." In Tobit, he ministered to a blind man. Oh my goodness. I'd been reading to Josiah about a blind man when all this started. The article described the angel as sometimes appearing with a greenish glow and wearing a green-colored sash to represent healing.

Josiah paced the floor making high-pitched squeals.

"Hey, bud, I have another question. Did Raphael happen to be wearing any particular color—other than white, I mean?"

**Green**, he typed.

I felt a mix of dread and excitement. What was this all about? Had God sent his angel Raphael to show us healing was on its way? It all sounded so farfetched and out of the box. Heaven forbid if I should tell anybody. But he'd had a huge communication breakthrough, so I had to at least tell his therapists.

By now, Kim, Keri, and Nicole had all left Partners, and Josiah hadn't yet bonded with Kay, his new senior therapist. Also, he was still trying to get used to Cassie. I'd talked to them about our success with RPM, but they couldn't use it at Partners because they had to follow a preset structure for insurance purposes.

"JoJo, what are you going to tell them at Partners?"

**I could give them pointers. How they can try different things.**

"Yes, you sure could."

I gathered my things to leave, but Josiah wanted to type something else.

**Quiet.**

"What do you mean, *quiet*? We're just about to go. Have you thought more about what you'd like to tell the therapists?"

He didn't hesitate. **Josiah is smart.**

"Yes, that's a very good thing to say. That's exactly what they need to know."

When Josiah and I arrived at Partners, we stepped into the lobby and I asked the receptionist if Kay and Cassie were available.

"I'll check," she said. "Give me a second, and I'll get them."

I fidgeted as I stared at the large room with its chairs, coffee table, book nook, toy area for kids, and a tin geometric art piece hanging on the wall.

Kay and Cassie stepped in, and I talked excitedly. "We had a big breakthrough this weekend."

"Oh, really?" Kay said. "What's up?"

"Josiah's writing full sentences on his iPad. It just happened."

Cassie's eyes widened. "Wow. We'd love to see that."

"Josiah, come here and show them what you can do." I held him, excited for what would be the ultimate show-and-tell. Instead he broke loose and ran for the wall, where he wildly tapped on the tin art.

"Come on!" I said, pulling him back. But as soon as I planted him on the chair, he curled his head into a headstand.

"Josiah, please. This way. Good. Now stay. What would you like to do first thing this morning?" I moved his arm to the iPad. "Go ahead, JoJo." But he didn't move. "Aren't you going to type something?" He looked blank, like nobody was home, and he refused to move a finger. "Show them how smart you are."

Kay closed her eyes, set a hand on my shoulder, and cleared her throat. "Sometimes parents want something so badly that they actually project it on their child."

Liquid heat coursed through my veins. She didn't believe me. She thought I was making this up. Like I'd really do that to my child.

"Look," I said, "I haven't projected any of this. It really happened, and it's still happening. He's just being stubborn."

Kay nodded. "It's okay."

No, it wasn't okay, and neither were their looks of pity.

"C'mon, Josiah," Cassie said. "Time to jump on the trampoline. Wave goodbye to your mom."

I rubbed my temples as I dragged myself to the car. I wanted to crawl into bed and have a good cry. Even more, I wanted to wring that dear boy's scrawny little neck. How could he do this to me? I went from the mountaintop of a communication miracle to utter humiliation. These people mattered to me, but they'd passed it off as a figment of my imagination.

When Joe returned from vacation, he saw the miracle firsthand. He watched Josiah type with his pointer finger as I anchored his arm, and he couldn't deny this incredible gift God had given us.

One chilly November night, Josiah poked his head out from under my covers like a turtle and typed, **age of healing.**

"What are you talking about? Who told you about the age of healing?"

**An angel.**

"I see. What do you need healing for?"

**Autism.**

I let out a long sigh. "How will you be healed?"

**Eager man.**

"Okay ... Who is the eager man?"

**Lamb.**

"Lamb what?" I fastened my eyes to the screen.

**Taste and see that God loves us.**

Playing dumb, I said, "How do we do that?"

**Satan is not the last man on a mission.**

"Who is then?"

**Angels of healing on a mission. Race for mankind. Satan laughs. Not on God's watch.**

Words, normal ones, strange ones, all kinds of ones, began to shoot out of him like water from a fountain. As much as I didn't want to miss anything, I had to go to Arizona to perform my niece Kriste's wedding.

My late brother's daughter looked striking in her long white gown. I'd met her six-foot-nine groom at Dean's funeral, and I enjoyed getting to know him during their pre-marriage counseling on Skype.

After the wedding, relatives wanted to hear about Josiah.

"That's amazing," said my brother Shane.

The support felt good, and I appreciated seeing my mom. She had remarried and now lived in Washington.

Mom grabbed my hands as we sat in the airport, preparing to say goodbye. "God isn't finished with this miracle, Tahni. He who began a good work in you will be faithful to complete it."

In my last minutes at the airport, I scurried like a squirrel, eager to find a gift for Josiah. With a brief time left before boarding, I quickly purchased a little plastic lizard and shoved it in my purse.

When I returned home, Joe greeted me in the kitchen and fell into my arms.

"Wow, I'll have to go away more often. It's good to see you too. How's the little guy? Is he downstairs?"

"Yup, in the sensory room."

I'd missed Josiah, but now that I'd returned I missed him even more. I longed for the words, "Mommy, Mommy, I missed you!" But when I walked over to where he stood on the mini trampoline, he didn't even register my face.

"I love you, JoJo. Here, I brought you a gift." I slipped the lizard in his hand, but he threw it to the floor. Not because he didn't want it, but because his brain didn't know how to process the new gift.

When I checked on him a few hours later, I found him back in his sensory room banging on his head.

"Why do you hit your head like that?"

**To quiet other sounds**, he wrote.

"I see you brought your lizard. What would you like to name him?"

**Opie hans.**

I chuckled. "That's great. Almost sounds like a German lizard. What made you choose that name?"

**Many lizards mate many mates but danasi lizards mate for life.**

I tried to swallow. "Okay. Who taught you about lizards?"

He pinched his nose. **Jesus educates me in school.**

I stared at him. "Um, what else do you know about lizards?"

**Lizards' pores are not just scales or aspiration scales, but many nodules on their skin.**

"Uh, anything else?"

**Lizards have ageless tails.**

"Joooe!" I hollered as I ran up the stairs. "We need to research lizards!"

The two of us sat side by side on our iPod and iPad, searching for facts.

After fifteen minutes, I asked, "Did you learn anything about that specific type of lizard?"

Joe shook his head. "No, but I found out about their tails. Listen to this. When attacked by a predator, a lizard can lose his tail and run away, distracting the predator by his still-moving body part. Lizards drop their tails when they sense danger, and they are able to grow them right back again."

"Wow," I said. "Sounds like an ageless tail to me. According to the article I found, there are reptiles in Australia that mate monogamously with the same individual for twenty years."

Joe rubbed his temples. "How does he know this kind of stuff?"

"I don't know. I haven't told him anything, and they sure don't teach these kind of details at Partners. They're more about drills and identification."

The following month, when Partners had their Christmas party, I wanted to create a good memory and maybe gloss over the humiliating show-and-tell fiasco.

I smiled at parents as their kids threw themselves into games and festivities. Josiah distanced himself and didn't join in on the fun. Why did he look so lost—like a fish that had been dropped in a foreign tank? It's one thing to be different from typical kids, quite another to be different from atypical kids.

"What did you think of Santa Claus?" I asked when we returned home.

Josiah typed, **He looks like Noah.**

I chuckled, assuming he'd seen Noah in a picture book. "So what did you like best about the party?"

**Riding in my mink stole. Riding in Jesus' sleigh to the new heaven high above terrain over the mountains.**

*Mink stole and sleigh?* Either he'd mixed up Jesus and Santa, or he'd expanded his supernatural experiences into the daytime hours.

A couple days later, Joe read to him about a blind boy who learned to play the piano. I followed it up with a talk about Temple Grandin, a brilliant woman with autism who processed information in pictures.

"Hey, JoJo, do you think in pictures too?"

**Not just in pictures or in sounds, but in total stories.** He started banging his hand against the window.

"Hey, stop it, would ya?"

But he kept at it. I probably said "stop" half a dozen times before he actually did.

"Josiah, why didn't you stop when I asked?"

**To test your will.**

I sighed. "Well, at least you're honest. Say, I've been thinking about all these amazing things you write. I'm wondering how you know how to spell like this. Can you tell me?"

**Jesus taught me the order of sounds.**

I sat dumbfounded. Not that I doubted God's ability. He could do anything. But I'd never heard of this. It almost sounded like some kind of heavenly Hooked on Phonics.

"Honey, did Jesus tell you other things?"

**Jesus said to remember not to test Satan.**

"How do you test Satan?"

**By doing naughty things.**

"Well, you better not test him then."

Josiah lifted his hand as if contemplating another window slap.

"Uh-uh," I said. "I asked you to be respectful and not to bang. We need to build trust, remember? Please say you're sorry."

**I'm sorry. At a future time I will behave.**

"JoJo, I love that you can communicate like this. It's amazing."

**I'm happy that I can allow you into my mind.**

Over the Christmas break, Josiah had a blast pushing buttons and feeling the texture of his new Dora the Explorer book.

"Nice gift from Grandma and Grandpa, isn't it? Hey, I have a treat for you. I'm going to read to you from your new Dora book as you eat vanilla ice cream."

"La, la, la, lee," he said, relishing one of his favorite repetitive sounds.

"Okay, here we go." I unleashed my best, more dramatic Spanish accent for Dora and Diego. Joe's laughter shot out from the bathroom.

"Hey, hope you're enjoying us from in there!"

I cleaned Josiah's face and hands. "So what did you think of the story?"

"Mmm," he said, typing. **Mom's story was too distinct. Not how you say true Spanish.**

I laughed. "Exactly how do you know what true Spanish sounds like?"

**Remembered some worshipers yelled really loud in heaven.**

There, he'd done it again. He wrote about heaven. Was he hallucinating? Either way, I needed to get to the bottom of this.

One night, early into the new year, Josiah got out of bed because he couldn't sleep.

"Okay, buddy," I said, nestling beside him on the blue couch. "What's so important that it can't wait?"

**God is opening up to me worlds gone by. Worship gave Lucifer great pride. God had opened access to a good world and not a naughty government.**

My mind reeled. "Josiah, why do you keep waking up in the night?"

**Lately a man has been nagging me awake.**

"Okay … A good man or a bad man?"

**Good angel.**

"Um … what does he say or do?"

**He takes me to various places in heaven.**

"Honey, I really don't understand this. It's all wonderful and amazing, but is there anything else you need to talk about?

Otherwise, I'd really like to get some sleep and try to make sense of this in the morning."

**Dad is depressed. Care for him.**

I stared from his words to his face. How did he know about his dad's little bout with depression? We'd never even talked about it in front of him.

A couple weeks later, Josiah came home teary-eyed from Partners.

"JoJo, why are you crying?"

**A father obligation after hanging around and not trying very hard to make haste on many fast angels and capitalizing on a good opportunity and . . .**

"Josiah, wait! Please don't keep running off. Come back. You need to finish." I pulled him back over.

**Dad is depressed and is not doing anything about it each day, and I can't accept it.**

What next? This kept getting wilder by the second. "Okay, it's time for our lesson. Let's go to the dining room."

I talked to Josiah about tropical fish. Then I grabbed the Children's Bible and read to him about the soldier who needed Jesus to heal his servant. "Josiah, what did the soldier need Jesus to do?"

**I remember Jesus told me about all matters of healing for the purpose of worship. Each motive is assessed for healing.**

"Okay," I said, fanning my face. What in the world had my son gotten into?

# 11

# Song of Heaven

"Sing like an overcomer."

– Josiah Cullen

*February 2013*

One chilly night, Josiah stormed into our room and woke us with a flick of the light.

"What's up?" I asked, steering him to the living room.

**Gog. Magog. A guarantee of a ministry of magnificent natural healing and an age of great advancement over autism. Age of healing.**

"Huh?" I was suddenly awake. "What's this about Magog?"

**Danger to peace. Fog in Magog. Last danger name is pestilence for men.**

I'd heard about Gog and Magog in the Bible, but I really didn't know much about them. A quick search on my iPad brought me to Ezekiel 38 where God defended Israel from her cruel enemy, Magog. Heaviness crept in. What kind of dark battle pictures had God been showing my child? And *why* was he showing them?

"JoJo, what do you think God wants you to know by giving you this?"

**He was guaranteeing my worship ministry. Fantastic story of God's love.**

Worship ministry for my son who couldn't speak, let alone

sing? I knew zip about music. Joe had played the saxophone in high school, but I hadn't inherited the music gene.

Still, I pondered Josiah's words about worship ministry. One day when Joe and I peeked around the corner and saw him pounding his toy lion piano and humming, "ah, ah, ah," we knew we had to sign him up for piano lessons.

Joe found Erin, a music therapist who gave lessons in a basement studio of an old remodeled home. A studio that Josiah perceived more like a jungle gym of stairs with easy access to kitchen faucets and fun-looking instruments. He stomped around like a bull in a china shop.

Whenever he grew restless during a lesson, he darted up the stairs, flung open the waiting room door, and made loud unmusical noises. I guess that's why it didn't surprise me after his second lesson when Erin wanted to talk to us.

"Josiah's quite the guy," she said.

Joe grinned. "That he is."

"Did you know he has perfect pitch?"

I looked at Joe. "Uh, no, actually we didn't."

"Yeah, a lot of parents boast that their kids have perfect pitch when they don't, but Josiah really does. Not only does he hum on pitch, but when I started playing the guitar, he put his hand on mine to stop me from playing. Then he plucked a string and ran over to the piano to play the same note so he could show me that my string was out of tune."

"How is that possible?" I said. "Nobody has ever taught him music."

A few lessons later, Erin approached us again. "Could you tell me more about Josiah? I'm working on my masters in psychology, and I've worked with a lot of kids with autism. Something is really different about your son. He doesn't present in the typical ways

I'm used to. What I'm saying is … I'd love to know what's going on behind those big blue eyes."

I fidgeted, trying to think fast. Nobody had ever asked us this before. "Erin, are you a Christian by any chance?"

"My family's Catholic. I go to church on holidays."

I blew out a breath. "Before I share with you, I want you to know a couple things. First, I'm a very stable person. I'm not on drugs or anything. And, Josiah isn't taking any medications."

"Go on."

"Okay. We don't know how, but we think Josiah is sometimes seeing through spiritual eyes. In September he had a communication breakthrough. Ever since then, he's been typing about angels and all kinds of wild things. We think he might be having some kind of heavenly experiences."

She raised an eyebrow. "Really … What do you think inspired all this? I mean, does he watch a lot of movies and TV? Read science fiction perhaps?"

"No, he's only seen a few kids' music videos, and he just recently saw his first sensory-friendly animated film. That's it."

"Hmm, I don't mean to probe, but did anything traumatic happen that might have caused him to disconnect from reality?"

I folded my arms. "No. Autism is the only traumatic thing that's ever happened to him. He has a stable home, and he's always been at the same trusted daycare and therapy center."

"Fascinating," she said. "If it's okay with you, I'd like to see something he's written. Maybe we could do something with it. I'd also like to get my supervisor's opinion."

The next day as I sat with Josiah on the couch, I approached him about it. "Would you like to write a song that you and Erin could work on together?"

I lightly propped his arm, and he moved his finger across the iPad without hesitation.

Mom, I give you this gentle, fun candle song that is centuries old. The legend is that it was sung each year by feminine gems. It is beamed to you, dear Mom. Peace for you. Leaping ways leap to victory.

**Peace I call**
**To no fear**
**Paths are clear**
**Battle is won**
**Band is here**
**Pitch your tent**
**Beam is clear**
**Fear not**

I sent him back with that song. His giftedness blew her away, but somehow the music Josiah heard on the inside didn't quite match what Erin came up with on the outside. When this happened more than once over a few months, Josiah couldn't hide his frustration, and it regularly earned him a spot on her timeout chair.

It didn't make sense. Here we'd cracked open a hidden world of words, but the efforts to put them to music only fell flat.

So when Erin took her maternity leave, we decided to move on too. The emotional and physical expense wasn't worth the constant headaches. Besides, we had enough challenges to concentrate on—like Josiah's first dentist appointment.

Josiah's occupational therapist had been desensitizing him to an electric toothbrush, so we figured we could pull off a checkup without sedation.

*Don't worry,* I told myself as I walked into the dentist's office. *You're prepared.* I had selected a lady dentist who came highly recommended for kids with special needs. I'd given Josiah all the pep talks, and Joe had read to him from *The Berenstain Bears Visit the Dentist.* I mean, what more could we do, right?

But the nightmare began as soon as the hygienist helped him

in the chair. He screamed bloody murder, jumped out, and yanked on the door.

"Stop!" I yelled.

The dentist shook her head. "I think we need to put him on a board and Velcro his hands, feet, and legs."

I stared at her. "Velcro him?"

"Don't worry, it won't hurt. We've done it lots of times."

Ignoring my churning stomach, I helped fasten him to the board.

"All is well," the dentist said.

But when she pried open his mouth, his leg broke free. He went on a kicking spree, wild and out of control.

"I need help over here!" she shouted.

Three assistants wrestled him down while he fought back. They refastened him, and everything stayed fine—for thirty seconds. To keep Josiah's mouth open, the dentist stuck a big metal instrument behind his teeth. He chomped on it so hard that he broke the hinge.

*God, this is my son. Not a psychiatric patient!*

"You're fine, JoJo," I said, hiding my tears. "It's okay. It's okay."

They gave him the world's fastest cleaning, sticking in the toothbrush between all his openings and closings.

"I'm sorry. I'm sorry," I told everybody. I glanced at the onlookers in the waiting room, who quickly returned to their phones and magazines.

Despite such ongoing mishaps, Josiah's writings continued to accelerate in leaps and bounds. One day I returned home from work, exhausted but with heaven on my mind.

"JoJo, can you do something for me?" I said, settling beside him in the kitchen. "If I give you the first line of a song, could you please finish it? It goes like this: 'My favorite place in heaven is …'"

His response came out in a downpour:

**My favorite place in heaven is over peaceful waters**
**Peace is real, tired souls naturally test peace**

**Roses are so stunning, worship the King**
**Sing loud to the prized pardon who requires praise**
**Angels taste of his holiness, ordained great attitude of praise**
**Help us worship the Lord together; please him**
**All you hail the King of majesty forever**
**Make a noise to the King on the throne.**

A sweet sense of God's presence filled the room, leaving me almost breathless, as words from the book of Revelation flooded my thoughts: *Holy, holy, holy, are you, Lord God Almighty. Worthy of all glory, honor, and praise.*

I hurried to call my mom. "Hey, I need to read you something."

When I finished the last line, peace and excitement hovered between us.

"Oh, Tahni, he's been there," she said. "He's been to heaven."

## 12

# Divine Directives

"Like a sparrow, rise up under God's best care."

– Josiah Cullen

**March 2013**

I didn't know whether to blame it on overtiredness, busyness, or just plain old stress, but I double-booked a meeting at work, and couldn't stop beating myself up over it.

Joe looked at me sympathetically. "You're fine. Could you please pass the salt?"

Nice attempt at comfort, but I still felt like a ditz. Of course, it didn't help that lately I'd been buried at work under the nuts and bolts of budgets and paperwork, making my job feel more practical than pastoral.

Josiah crammed a piece of chicken in his mouth and swatted the table.

"How was Partners?" I asked, clearing a spot for his iPad.

**It was a party in pod ten. I fanned a fun revolt with a fart feast and offended my red-haired friend. I like to feel fast, fun farts. Lead me to beans!**

I cupped my mouth. "Hear that, Joe? He's definitely his father's son."

Joe set down his glass. "Buddy, you come from a long line of gas men."

"Whatever," I said. "Josiah, you're wiggly. What do you say we move to the couch?"

Shifting pillows, I nestled beside him. "Hey, I'd love to hear what's on your mind."

"Eeeeee," he said as his finger went down. **Mistook sloppy times. Quit ongoing issues of nuts and bolts. Pride goes before a fall. So tell your pastor time for you to get on a new path in life. Even tell wise people. Be prudent in last month in having a mission statement.**

**It is essential others know. Sell yourself. Eat diet food. Love life. Make a plan. Argue new strong leads of quiet moms. Repair marriage. Tell mothers to quit pleading, to rise up in victory.**

"Whoa," I said, trying to absorb it. "That's a lot." I stared in amazement at *nuts and bolts*. Josiah had practically read my mind! And as far as getting on *a new path in life*, did he mean leaving my job? Uh, I don't think so. Not when I bring home half the bacon.

How in the world did my seven-year-old come up with all this? Did God want to use him to get my attention? If so, Josiah might be right to highlight that *pride goes before a fall*. Especially since I had a tendency to think I kept the family afloat.

As far as him writing *tell wise people* … well, I would definitely have to do that. I'd be crazy to move forward on this kind of a word without confirmations.

That part about *having a mission statement*? Sheesh! It sounded like I was supposed to tell them why I'd be leaving. Well, I wanted to be more available for my family.

*Eat diet food.* Seriously? What little boy would say that kind of thing to his mother? Either one who was looking for trouble, or one who happened to see life from a whole different perspective.

*Argue new strong leads of quiet moms.* That actually made sense to me, because no matter what happened with my job, I'd already resolved to keep helping mothers online.

*Repair marriage.* My heart sank. Each weekend I worked four services at Spring Lake Park, and soon it would be five. I oversaw a special needs ministry, and I'd just heard I might be asked to supervise the operations team, which would drain our family time even more. *Tell mothers to quit pleading, to rise up in victory.* What? Did God want me to sound a battle cry and tell mothers to lose a victim mentality? If so, I'd have to lose mine first.

I patted Josiah's shoulder. "Thanks. This is incredible. How about you go play?"

I rushed to my room and collapsed on my bed with the phone. "Mom, we need to pray." I could hear the intensity in my voice as I explained what happened.

Mom broke into a passionate prayer asking God for wisdom and discernment.

"Do you sense anything about this?" I asked.

"Yes, I think so," she said. "I think Josiah's words are a clear message from God."

Next I sought advice from my friend Donna, a soulful woman I'd met several years back at a Relevance Conference. Donna had recognized me from a photo in our church magazine. As we introduced ourselves, I learned that her daughter had autism too. She knew Keri from Partners before Keri became the director. Apparently, Keri used to be Donna's daughter's in-home ABA therapist. Small world. And after the conference, Donna and I began to enjoy periodic get-togethers in her gorgeous country home.

"Leave your job?" she said. "Do you feel God's peace about that? I mean, do you think the Holy Spirit might be preparing you for a new season? He knows our hearts. I really don't think you need to worry though, because God honors us when we step out in obedience."

"Thanks," I said, gazing out her picture windows that overlooked a valley of trees. "That's just what I needed to hear."

I talked to my Bethel buddy, Michele, who had become a new person since our glory trip.

"Oh, I love what he wrote," she said. "Just think how much it would benefit Josiah to have you home more often. It only makes sense."

Now I just needed to talk to Joe. If he said no, I might as well forget the whole thing.

It turned out he had to work late that night, so I decided to get a head start on my resignation letter.

First I wrote Steve. Then I thanked Pastor Bob, Scott, and the whole management team.

*Thank you for the last thirteen life-changing years at Eagle Brook. Thank you for taking a chance on me and raising me up to learn how to lead, grow in Christ, and be part of a team that's focused on reaching others for the kingdom.*

The next morning I met Joe's gaze across the table. "Josiah gave me a word."

"Oh? What about?"

"My job." I shoved the iPad in front of him. "He wrote about me leaving. Apparently, God has a new path for me, and it would allow me to be at home more."

Joe brought his finger to his chin. "Well, if you stayed home, I'm not sure that would solve things as much as you think. On the other hand, I doubt we'd ever regret being more available for Josiah."

I grabbed his hands. "I know this would drastically bite into our finances, but I've calculated my accumulated paid time off, and if we pool together all our savings, we'll have enough to last through the summer. Then maybe down the road God will open up some freelance work or another ministry opportunity."

Joe studied me. "Why don't we think about this over the weekend and write out the pros and cons?"

"Okay, and why don't we pray about it?"

"Sure. Go ahead."

"Father God, we need direction and clarity. Please keep Joe and me on the same page. We want your wisdom and your will, no matter what happens. In Jesus' name."

"Amen," said Joe. "I don't like stepping out into the unknown, but if this is something you feel strongly about, I'll support you. I know you don't just step into something without carefully considering it. So if you think you need to quit, we'll find a way to make it work."

Four days later, I was up for my mid-year review. I knocked on Pastor Steve's door, pushing my resignation letter deep in my purse.

"Hey, Tahni. Come in and have a seat." He smiled from across his desk. "You do these kinds of reviews with your team. Now it's your turn to hear me say wonderful things about you." He slid the paperwork in front of me. "We've given you high scores across the board. We like how you conduct yourself with both your team and the congregation. It's been an intense season, but you've really hit your stride in leadership. Fabulous job."

"Wow, I'm honored. Thanks."

"You're welcome. Also, we'd like to give you a raise."

My throat went dry. "Really? I never expected this." I fingered the resignation letter, which suddenly felt sweaty.

"Well, you deserve it."

"Hmm, I really don't know how to say this." I pulled out the envelope. "I came here planning to turn in my resignation."

"Oh? Everything okay?"

"Yeah, it's great. But the Lord seems to be leading me in a different direction."

He sat back in his chair. "Wow, I didn't see that one coming."

"Neither did I."

"Would you like to talk about it?"

"Sure. You probably remember how I shared with you that Josiah suddenly started communicating?"

"Yes, it's amazing how he really took off with it."

"Well, you might find this hard to believe, but God actually used his communication to influence my decision. That's why Joe and I feel we need to step out in obedience."

He rested his head on his hand. "You'll leave a big pair of shoes to fill. That's for sure. But if God says go, then you go.

"When God called my wife and me to leave a church and start a new one, it felt completely unreasonable. God confirmed it though, so we moved to Colorado. My wife was nervous, as you can imagine. We didn't know how we'd feed the family, but you know what I said? I told her that even if God gets us through winter on beans and onions, he'll help us make it.

"So we arrived in our new Colorado neighborhood, and I ended up going door-to-door inviting people to church. This rough-looking guy in a trailer told me he wanted to give me something. He took me around to the storage in the back—and guess what he pulled out?"

"What?"

"A fifty-pound bag of dry beans and a huge sack of onions."

"No way."

"Yeah way. The guy told me, 'Here you go. These ought to get you through the winter.'"

I laughed. "That's crazy."

"Exactly. I told my wife I should have said, 'God will provide steak all winter.' But it all worked out."

Chuckling, I silently thanked God for another confirmation.

During my few remaining weeks on the job, my church friends and staff went out of their way to tell me what a difference I'd made in their lives. They gave me notes and gifts, including a family membership to the zoo. Somehow God allowed me to wrap up all my loose ends. I made a farewell video for the congregation. God even let me squeeze in a baptism and some back-to-back Easter services.

On my last day, the staff threw me a party. Baby Gracie's mother,

Becky, provided cupcakes. My team showed a video they made in my honor. Then we sealed it all up the way it began—with prayer.

I instantly loved the extra time with Josiah.

One day, after a good romp on the trampoline, he typed, **I feel I need a gab.**

I laughed. "Okay, let's gab. Race you to the couch."

And he knew right what he wanted to say:

**Each time I gab, tons of inspiring quotes are said. Nutty to me that you don't post them on Facebook.**

*He* found it nutty that I didn't share all this nuttiness on my Facebook page? Did he even have a clue what people might think of me if I posted his words? Then I had a thought.

"Josiah, you're right. Your words could really bless people. Maybe I could make a special page just for you. That way I could feature your insightful quotes and poems. Family and friends could join if they wanted."

**Perfect idea. Love it, Mom.**

I smiled. "What do you want to call it?"

**Josiah's picture it done.**

Well, I didn't want to hurt his feelings, but that one wouldn't fly. I thought for a moment and remembered how when he used to have night terrors I would sing over him the meaning of his name. "The fire of the Lord is upon you. The fire of the Lord is upon you now." Josiah meant "fire of the Lord," so why not call the page "Josiah's Fire"?

"About your Facebook page," I said. "If we're really going to do this, I think you're going to need to take a big step and start thinking about learning to write without me supporting your arm. Do you understand?"

**Picture it done. Healing comes in me. Jesus wants left gun function prayed over in me. Nudged to pray for it.**

"Okay. Well, in Jesus' name, I speak to the left lobe of your brain and to all those transistors that trigger function. I pray they fire with clarity and accuracy. I bind any interference. I speak peace into that left lobe and call it whole in Jesus' name. There. How was that?"

**Worth a picture of party. Faith is learning to praise for a healing.**

"In that case," I said, "let's turn on the music."

And he rocked back and forth to the beat.

Later in the night, he tripped into my room all upset.

"Shh," I said. "Don't wake Daddy."

Josiah knew the routine. I grabbed my glasses and followed him to the living room. "What's up, sweetie? Why did you wake me?"

**Please pacify best boy. I was cold. On former nights I went to bed warmly. Will you put pants on me please? My head is feeling bent toward really ghastly feels of pent-up rage, and I feel quite bad. Make it gap closed. Pray for peace, please.**

Passion rose up inside me. "Okay. Father, you hear Josiah's heart. Please give him peace. Take away all this pent-up frustration. Thank you for being big enough to handle our emotions. We ask you to rule his thoughts and make them only for you. In Jesus' name."

But Josiah woke me up a second time.

"What now?" I asked.

**Auntie packed an idea. Call it Peace Café. Dare peaceful fun family. Picture it done.**

**Padded pockets fund it. Back in best mom's focused heart under her beaming café. Baptize it in peace. Yes, Grandma. Quite a Jesus fest. Café is pie and coffee like she dreamed of. Picture it done.**

**Gifts are caring representations of Jesus peace. Kiss me now. Peace is fun. Gem is lunging fun money Grandma's way. Auntie is pie in the sky.**

"Wait—you're talking about my mom, your grandma, right? Are you saying she's supposed to start some kind of a café and sell gifts? What kind of gifts?"

**Peaceful items of Grandma's to make and buy. Bible studies are part of it. Pass it on to her. It is legendary.**

**In Washington, peace is being spread. Hope is being spread. It is party time. Party is Mary's family. Party is Rusty's family. It is heavenly inheritance. It is pie in the sky.**

**I model peace to hopeful Mom. Obey Jesus. Net gain is taste of heaven. Just believe. Tell each need to Jesus.**

As soon as eight o'clock Washington time rolled around, I called my mom to share Josiah's words. "I know. I don't know what to make of it either, but get this. He mentions people in heaven like Grandma Mary and Grandpa Rusty. I'm telling you, this is crazy."

After Mom thought about it for a couple days, she called me back. "I haven't owned a shop in over twelve years and I'm happily retired, so I think Josiah was referring to a principle rather than to an actual physical place. Maybe I'm supposed to get more involved in Bible studies and start serving people."

"Oh my goodness, Mom. This is going to blow you away. I need to read you what Josiah just typed before you called."

**Feel gregarious café is merely an idea, but it is a place of business. Bask, dear Sharon, I call it Peace Café. Obedient peace is calling. Baptize it in peace. Fabulous passion is ignited. Cares pass over.**

**Picture it done, and I call it a deal. Funds beam to make it possible. Cast your cares on me, Jesus says, for I care for you, family.**

"Hello? Mom? Are you still there?"

"Yeah, I'm here."

"Well, what do you think?"

"I think that if this is what God wants me to do, I'm certainly open to it. I never felt a sense of completion when I walked away from past businesses. So if God provides the finances like Josiah says he will, then this could be a good thing. We'll just have to move forward and see what God does."

# 13

# How God Sees Us

"A round pearl is troubling to you only if trouble
does not leave your shell in beauty."
– Josiah Cullen

*May 2013*

"Guess what, JoJo? You and Daddy get to go to your first ever sensory-friendly play. It's called *Beauty and the Beast*. I saw the movie many years ago and I think you're really going to like it. Please just remember to keep your hands to yourself and sit nice, okay?"

Josiah vibrated his lips and slapped the kitchen table near my orange juice.

"I wish I could be with you," I said, "but I accepted this free conference ticket a while ago, and Daddy just heard about the play. So what do you think?"

**Help me face a fear. Answer a happy peace question before Dad pads it. Far, far feline is a garish, dapper boyfriend or a gutsy fiend? I can't tell.**

Far feline? What was he talking about? The Beast? If I remembered correctly, the Beast did look a little cat-like. He seemed one way and turned out to be another. How could Josiah know this when he'd never seen the movie?

"Hey, Josiah. How do you know what *Beauty and the Beast* is about?"

**Cabaret is prophetic to autism. Story plays out in real life. I am helping Dad find peace in life. Destiny is princely.**

Holy moly! Five days ago, Josiah had written something about an "autism cabaret," relating to healing and change. We didn't even know about this musical for kids with autism back then. Was it possible Josiah had seen the play in his spirit? No, it couldn't be, but what did he mean about Joe finding peace?

"JoJo, I'm sure Dad would want to know about *Beauty and the Beast* being prophetic to autism. Should I tell him now or wait until after he sees the play?"

**Before is much better. Gears are about opening it to peace and healing past autism effects on my mind. Gifts are being sent.**

He darted off, and at the same time Joe waltzed over in his pajamas. "Good morning, babe."

"Joe, you're not going to believe this."

"What, we're out of my favorite Eggo waffles again?"

"No. Well, that too, but this is about Josiah. He's never seen the *Beauty and the Beast* movie, but I think he knows what it's about and he says the story is prophetic to autism."

Joe's eyebrows arched up. "Whoa. That's weird."

"I know. Do you think it's possible he somehow saw it in his mind? Beforehand, I mean?"

Joe pursed his lips. "Well, I suppose anything is possible."

"Listen, I'm running late for my conference, but can you please do me a big favor? I need you to keep a close eye on that play and try to watch it through a new lens. Can you do that?"

"Sure. Have fun with the ladies."

The women's conference featured an all-chick band. After one of the songs, the worship leader told us to "encourage someone nearby. Try to be sensitive to the Holy Spirit."

A gray-haired lady placed her hand on my shoulder and leaned close. "I have a word for you."

My heart quickened. "Okay, go ahead."

"I see you standing strong and sounding a silver trumpet. I hear a new voice. A voice that is going to make waves and break open the atmosphere. A voice with an announcement that makes major tremors across the land."

I held my hand to my chest. Josiah. Did this mean he would be healed and start to talk?

I thought about her words all through lunch.

When I returned and took my seat, the speaker scanned the audience from left to right. "God likes to surprise us. Sometimes we think one thing is going to happen, but God shakes our plans and hands us something even better. I'd planned a full PowerPoint presentation, but God just impressed on my heart that he wants me to share a completely different message."

*Brave woman*, I thought. *Especially in a crowd of eight hundred women who have high expectations.*

"If your identity is in a circumstance or in another human being," she said, "you are believing a lie. You need to rest in who you are: the daughter of the Most High God.

"Ladies, he calls us to be a living sacrifice. That means we are dead to our flesh. I would like to do something a little bit different today. The worship team is going to play some funeral music, and we are going to have a funeral processional. If you need to die to something so you can live, it's time to take a risk and step out. We're going to toss those harmful areas over to God and let him bury them once and for all."

Hundreds of women stepped out of their seats, and I knew God wanted to take me to the next level. I stepped out as the band played "Amazing Grace," and I knelt in front of the cross.

*Have your way, King Jesus. Highlight the places where I need to die. Help me think like royalty. I'm done with self-pity. Here's the key*

*to all my unruly emotions. Help me see life as you do. Take all my*
*hurt and make me new.*

During the dinner break, I called home. "How did he do during the play?"

"Fine. He went into the aisle and got a bit loud, but he watched it."

"So … did anything jump out at you in light of Josiah's word?"

"Well, to tell you the truth, I'm really not sure what I was
supposed to look for or get out of it. I didn't catch it all either. You
know how it is when you're trying to keep an eye on Josiah."

I felt my body tense. This was a test, and I recognized it. But no
way would I let the Enemy steal my joy from the conference.

When I came home, I crashed and didn't wake up until morning
when I heard a loud whirring noise from one of Josiah's toys.

"It's early," I said. "Don't wake up Daddy." Then I remembered
it was Joe's turn to catch the early church service. "Hey, buddy, want
to tell me about the play?" I took him to the living room couch and
sidled up beside him, so he could type.

**Dad is really tone deaf to spiritual things. Peace is the voice
of love for yourself. People are poaching interests of peace.**

He ran to the bathroom and came out with a wad of toilet
paper in his mouth.

"Hey, get back here." I gathered the shreds and tried to direct
him to the living room, but he dashed to the kitchen and climbed
on the counter. "Josiah, can you finish what you were writing?"

When I finally got him back to the couch, he wrote up a storm,
a whirlwind of spiritual parallels from *Beauty and the Beast*. In the
middle of each thought, though, he had to jump to his feet and
bounce like a wild thing on the couch.

"Josiah, I swear one of these days you're going to bust the
springs on this thing." Gently, I pulled him back down and watched
him start a new sentence.

**Jesus is very nice to look on himself as beautiful in every way. It was he who showed me all my natural pieces of the play nights before I ever saw it.**

Joe returned a few hours later. He looked at me in my thick glasses with my bed head and he chuckled. "Another lazy Sunday in the Cullen home, I see."

I stepped closer to him in the kitchen. "Joe, I have a serious question. Do you know if Gaston from the play had a hole in his sock?"

He raised an eyebrow. "Say what?"

"A hole in his sock. Think hard. Oh, and let me know if you remember anything about bats."

"Boy, you sure ask a lot of nitpicky questions."

"Okay, but Josiah has been writing about the play for over an hour—and not just about what he saw. He's making all kinds of deep spiritual connections. I really just want to know what he means."

"Hmm," he said. "Maybe we could find an old copy of the movie?"

"If we do," I eyed him hopefully, "will you watch it with me?"

"Sure, let's have a *Beauty and the Beast* date night."

I stayed in the car with Josiah while Joe ran into Half Price Books to look for the video. Just then, a green compact Honda parked in front of us, and I stared at its license plate. EGG 689. EGG stood out to me because of something Josiah typed after God asked me to leave my job: **Chickens work hard to produce eggs. Squirrels just gather nuts. Be a squirrel.** Ever since he wrote it, the word egg kept popping up all over the place. And 68 stood out because God had been leading me to Psalm 68. So for fun, I'd look up verse nine.

Joe opened the door. "They don't have it."

"Okay, let's try Savers. Can I borrow your phone to look up a verse?"

"Sudden inspiration?" he said, handing it over.

"Uh, you could say that. Check out that license plate. You know how I've been seeing 'egg' lately? Well, let's read the verse. Psalm 68:9. 'You gave abundant showers, O God; you refreshed your weary inheritance.'"

The instant I said the words, heavy rain poured from the sky.

Joe drew back. "Wow. Talk about a coincidence."

"More like a God-incident," I said. "He's so into the details. Lord, please send your abundant showers. Refresh your weary inheritance—us!"

We found a copy of the movie at Savers, and as soon as Josiah fell asleep, we settled in downstairs. I had a pen and a notebook in hand, eager to review Josiah's iPad comments.

**Autism, ADD, and ADHD fan fear. It is peace-damning, fabricating bats of irritation in kids.**

**Odd behavior and passivity are being introduced. In peace, faith is best perfected in facing it. Fearing it puts rage into our blessed lives. It causes a genetic ban on a best passion for life.**

**Jesus plans to fix it, ending fears. Measure your peace levels.**

The movie started, and the story's details sprung back to life. An enchantress placed a curse on a self-oriented young prince, changing him into an unruly beast. The prince's castle gave way to chaos, danger, despair, and fear. His servants turned into furniture caricatures, mere fractions of their old selves.

The frustrated Beast began to hate himself for his peculiarities. Having read Josiah's word, the prince's vices reminded me of the peace-robbing, fear-breathing effects of ADD and ADHD. They could make anyone in their home feel stuck and isolated.

*This is a battle we must face and win,* I wrote. *Jesus will fix it.*

I returned to Josiah's words.

**Jesus penned a play. Each daughter is generationally offered a partnership with Jesus, tapping past problems. For Beauty, like you, Mom, her pie in the sky is muddy. Play like a little girl. Please learn quickly. Healing comes.**

**Learning to love is a measly pursuit, but daring to beauty helps a person tell another person copious, festive things about love's purposes. Love is part friendship and part passion.**

Belle longed for love and adventure, but when her father became imprisoned in the castle, her ideals turned to mud. Belle found herself in the castle with the enemy where the enchanted servants encouraged her at a feast. Her choice to celebrate in the midst of her horrible situation brought emotional freedom, reviving her hope. Then Belle seized an opportunity to sacrificially offer herself as a prisoner in exchange for her father's freedom.

I nudged Joe, so he could read Josiah's words.

**Gaston feels less like the frantic feline. Baptized in Gaston's facets that are dashing and mature, men get called for festive, regal fun. His bare toe is a picture of the test passed.**

**Real men get feelings after Gaston set his feet up. Feet are a sense of feeling. They feel fast. It feels good. They feel slow, it feels bad.**

**God insists that fathers feel a party. A confident but more quiet spirit of manlihood presents a core of peace for the family. Men quit operating under it, but it is essential to family help. It is men totally committed to be godly in passion, love, and pictures of faith in really tough times.**

After Joe returned to the movie, he jerked back in surprise. "I saw it," he said. "Did you see that? Gaston's toe poking out. I don't think they did that in the play, but I saw it just now. Remarkable."

"I know. So if God showed us about the toe in Josiah's word, it must mean something significant." I jotted more notes.

Gaston had stuck his feet on the table and didn't care about the little things like a hole in his sock, but Josiah saw much more. He saw Gaston as a man on a mission, unmoved by distractions around him.

Personally, I'd seen Gaston as nothing but a jerk. Josiah's words, however, reminded me that if I looked deep enough, I could always find the gold in people. God made men to be jovial, strong, brave, and brimming with confidence.

After Belle rejected Gaston, his tavern buddies reminded him of his identity and he snapped out of his depression, regaining confidence. Likewise, we all wrestle with the Beauty and Beast inside. Wait. Hadn't Josiah tied the Beauty to Jesus? I had to check. **Pouting is not Jesus. He is beautiful. He is very joyful. He is very nice to look on himself as beautiful in every way. So he is noting you look only on his beauty, and you won't be like a beast.**

I thought about how Romans 8 described that we shouldn't be controlled by the sinful nature that leads to death. Instead, we should let the Holy Spirit control our minds and experience his fearless life and peace.

The more I read, the more I wondered how in the world Josiah had come to unpack all these deep mature themes.

**The beast fails to know a sense of peace. Like the beast, Dad is feeling fast like rabble, but his destiny is king. Since feeling bad about yourself regulates bad cells, name it a beast. Failing peace is beastly behavior.**

**Forgetting a party most times passes on the beast. Gaze on the daze. It is depression. Cells of abandonment and shame are a beast. Jealously is a beast. Thinking God is more about judgment and less about love is a beast. Pride is a beast. Everybody faces a beast.**

**God basks in total, positive men. Dad is a perfect, dashing prince. Don't Gaston it, but do party like Gaston in perfect, dapper peace. Tell Dad his peace is like Gaston's and your peace is like Beauty's. Live like it.**

Yikes. I'd have to show this one to Joe too. Hopefully, he'd focus on the positivity and reject the beastliness. Clearly, God wanted to release freedom, peace, and joy as we looked at life through his lens, not ours.

**Love is arguing with all the noise of your own judging of yourself and verifying all your humanity is already under his huge light.**

The Beast felt so far removed from his original identity as a prince that he couldn't even recognize himself anymore. He'd lost hope, so with his own two claws, he ripped up his old princely portrait.

But Belle began to treat the Beast with kindness, and he grew in so much confidence that he released her to go find her father.

As Belle ventured back out in the world, she refused Gaston's advances. This, of course, infuriated him, so he ordered the Beast to be killed. By now, Belle defended the Beast, claiming he'd been misunderstood.

Back in the castle, Belle and the Beast began a playful banter that sparked a new relationship. Shame and blame gave way to forgiveness, gratitude, openness, and vulnerability. They saw fresh beauty in each other. The smallest flicker of love managed to remove the Beast's fear and self-pity.

Wolves attacked Belle, but the Beast, enflamed by love, became willing to lay down his life for her.

The wounded Beast stood at death's door, but seconds before the last rose petal hit the floor, Belle confessed her love for him. Love broke the curse. The Beast and his household found themselves restored to their original kingdom design. Belle and the prince lived happily ever after.

I couldn't write fast enough: *We don't need to live like we're rejected. We are loved, forgiven, and accepted. Beastly thinking brings hurt and keeps us from being who we were made to be—God's royal heirs.*

Josiah had written a ton on this topic. In fact, I'd never seen him write so much.

**Celebration is a party of praise, healing past wounds, toasting to happy times. Peace positions positivity. Positivity positions praise. Praise positions purpose.**

**God is giving you a new fashion with angelic personality, Mom. Worship God in seamless, beautiful pearls. Playtime is here.**

**Beauty is presenting yourself worth seemingly millions.**

**It is essential to sit longer, imagining his presence. Please play princess games.**

**Jesus says, "I sear princess on your heart. It is peace for life, princess of peace. If the Father feels that way, demons don't steal your stuff. I lease my authority to you. Demonstrate full faith. Fun times are coming, Princess Tahni, Prince Joseph, Prince Josiah. I promise I provide for you. Peace."**

*Princess games.* I loved that. I marveled at how God wanted me to play them. Me, a former tomboy who used to hang with the guys, build forts, climb roofs, and play GI Joe.

*Good one, God.*

The final scene, when Belle danced with the Beast, reminded me of heaven's redemption. Everyone would be celebrating the way God described it in Psalm 30:11–12: "You have turned my mourning into joyful dancing. You have taken away my clothes of mourning and clothed me with joy, that I might sing praises to you and not be silent. O Lord my God, I will give you thanks forever!" (NLT).

A week later, I returned to Donna's beautiful country home. "What a feast," I said, enjoying her pasta and bruschetta.

"Josiah's words are a feast," she said. "I've never heard anything quite like them."

"That makes two of us," I said. "Ever since *Beauty and the Beast,* I've been trying to see myself as God sees me. Like his beautiful princess." I looked from her high ceiling to the valley of trees. "I've always struggled with weight issues. As a child, my grandma told me I looked hefty. 'Better not eat that candy!' "

Donna shook her head. "Sheesh, that's horrible."

"The funny thing is, I've looked at pictures of myself from back then, and I really don't think I was even big. Of course, that was before my dad came home with a barrel of candy he won by guessing the right amount. That junk filled our pantry for months."

Donna chuckled.

"So get this," I said. "Josiah typed something really interesting. He wrote that looking on God is big to your own beauty. Ok, let me get this right." I glanced at the iPad. "**God is our huge light on our bodies.**" I shook my head. "That boy. He has no idea."

"Wow," Donna said. "Your son's truths are life-changing."

"After he wrote that, I started a secret Pinterest board because I wanted to think about what it means to be a princess, a child of the King. I figured that seeing what my robe and crown might look like might help me be able to better grasp it spiritually."

Donna jumped to her feet. "Excuse me. I'll be right back."

When she returned, she hid something behind her back. "My mom's originally from the Philippines, so when I recently visited, I bought these earrings." She pulled them out. "I feel like God wants me to give them to you."

I gasped. "Oh my gosh, Donna. They're gorgeous. I can't believe it. Silvery green pearls. You need to see this." I pulled out my iPad and showed her my secret Pinterest board. "The pearls in your earrings are just like the silvery green pearls in this bracelet I pinned. I specifically chose this picture because these pearls are so unique. They made me feel like royalty, like the bride of Christ."

Donna beamed. "Sounds like somebody wants to give you a loud and clear message."

"Thanks," I said, giving her a hug. "Since God wants me to play princess games, I see these pearls as being from both you and him—and they're gorgeous."

"Just like you, Princess Tahni."

I chuckled. *Okay God, I get it. Let the princess games begin.*

# 14

# Tune to Joy

"Joy is not frightening to have
if joy is your honor to possess."
– Josiah Cullen

**Spring 2013**

I expected a normal drive home after an evening get-together with mothers of autistic children. But when I came to the I-94 Lowry Hill Tunnel near Minneapolis, I felt a flutter.

I'd passed through the tunnel more times than I could count. I was familiar with the four lanes, the thirty-five-mile-an-hour curve, and the bright lines of light. This time, though, when I reached the halfway point, something came over me, and I hyper-focused on the cement sides. I felt detached and out of control, gulping for air.

*I'm going to crash!* My heart pounded and heat saturated my body. I wanted out and felt trapped. *Breathe!* Adrenaline surged. Steady now. Don't swerve.

Sweat oozed out my pores as I held the wet steering wheel in a death grip. Sinking, pulsing, churning. *Keep going,* I told myself.

I pushed to the other side, relieved I'd made it through alive. Then I hyper-focused on the short cement slabs at the sides of the interstate. What if I hit them?

What was wrong with me? My brain went haywire in hyperdrive. This wasn't like me. Heavy traffic had never been a problem, and this wasn't even heavy traffic!

Tears burned and I felt sick. *Pull over*, I told myself. I took the next exit and collapsed on the steering wheel at a gas station, trying to breathe.

Finally, I went in to use the restroom and to buy a bottle of water for my parched throat.

*You'll be fine*, I told myself. When I buckled back in, fear knifed me all over again. What if this became my new reality? I'd just left a good job and had places to go. What if fear locked me up so tight that it sucked the life out of me? I'd heard of people gripped in a cycle of panic attacks, and I didn't want to be one of them.

I stayed off the main interstate and opted for the less-traveled residential roads. No matter how hard I tried, I couldn't shake off that out-of-control feeling that had stampeded my heart.

Finally, I pulled into my driveway. I minced into my quiet home and slid under the warm sheets next to Joe and his slow rhythmic breathing.

The next day, I had to take Josiah to a birthday party. I hadn't told Joe about what happened because I didn't want to worry him. The last thing I needed was to have him check up on me all the time.

Hearing Josiah's noises in the backseat made me feel an extra weight of responsibility. I did fine until I came to the bridge that connects Minnesota and Wisconsin. Then the nightmare began all over again.

*Tahni, hold it together for Josiah.* But my fight-or-flight mechanism wouldn't listen. *God, I need you. Helllp!*

My thoughts raced back to fear.

*God, you keep me in perfect peace. I fix my eyes on you.*

Thankfully, I made it through, but I couldn't go on like this.

Two days later, Josiah spilled his thoughts.

**Make a new application about heaven. Gates and robes. Fear is peace irrationalized. Men need to know it.**

I stared at him. "Josiah, that's quite an accurate definition of fear. Did you know I had a big test the other day when I was driving? I had something called a panic attack. Do you know what that is?"

**Seems pretty clear. Test functioned effectively.**

I sat stunned. "Josiah, what's a gate?"

His answer flew off his pointer finger. **A gate is in your mind, and it is in your way if it lands you outside the pastures of his care. You wander out if all you do is function on mind facts and not your safety inside his gates. Faith gets your mind to look on a legal affidavit of praise.**

"Affidavit of praise? What?"

**Don't pout. Just praise, Mom.**

"Honey, you make it sound so easy. Okay, so what's the significance of a robe?"

**It's a remnant obedient people wear doing beautiful things during daily decisions of faith. A robe is a remnant after God's righteousness. It lets you feel assets of God's goodness.**

"Where do you learn all this stuff? Is there a Bible passage about gates or something?"

**Benjamin's little tribe entered the first gate by looking to praise for his joy. It is in Judges. Ask me a question. Faith is fun. Best decision Benjamin makes is to fear God much more than man.**

"Okay, I'll check it out."

I did a search and parked on Judges 5. There I read Deborah's Song, which mentions how "war came to the city gates." Singers and musicians remembered God's victories as they marched. Even though Israel's largest tribes didn't participate in God's call to battle, the warriors of Benjamin along with three other tribes did. They stood victorious against impossible odds.

So Josiah was right when he said the little tribe of Benjamin trusted God more than they feared man. They put their lives on the line when they stepped out in obedience. But how did Josiah know all these things and where to find them in the Bible? And since when had he become my personal Bible teacher?

I started studying gateways and began to see them as key entryways and exits. In ancient times, people who possessed the gate possessed the city. They kept watchmen at the gates to keep their enemies out and their allies in.

Had I let the gates of my life be protected by God's covering, or had I inadvertently opened a door to the Enemy? I knew as a follower of Christ that I needed to guard all the gates of my eyes, mouth, ears, and emotions. I couldn't open myself to anything from the opposite kingdom, the one that hijacks our freedom.

Josiah's words about praise helped me see it as a spiritual weapon. I began to praise while driving, and the more I did, the more God drove out the spirit of fear. Sure, I still felt a slight twinge of fear from time to time, but God had given me a key to his gate of rational peace.

I treasured my times with God more than ever. One morning as I read about Mrs. Perfect in Proverbs 31, I came to verse 25 where she laughs at the days to come. Suddenly, I flushed in frustration. I'd never cared for the Barbie of the Bible, but this time she got to me more than ever. I stomped to the bathroom and stepped in the shower, ready to have it out with God.

*God, you want me to be a woman who laughs without fear of the future. Well, I want to know how I'm supposed to do that when you don't want me to be the Pollyanna-type who pretends everything's okay when it isn't. What do you want me to do—admit I'm afraid? Okay, I'm afraid!*

*I'm afraid about what will happen to Josiah. I'm afraid about our money situation. And I'm afraid about not having it all together in our marriage. There.*

Just then, something hit me: I was afraid of happiness. The realization nearly knocked me over, and I sobbed uncontrollably.

*Why am I afraid of happiness, God? I laugh all the time. I'm joyful and optimistic.*

I shut off the water and stepped out, heaving and dripping with tears.

God's words came to me: *You laugh, Tahni, but your laughter is guarded and suspicious like Sarah's when I told her she'd bear a child in her old age.*

I thought for a minute, and God reminded me I needed to learn from Sarah, who waited many years for her promised son, Isaac. I threw on some clothes and grabbed my Bible and commentary.

*Isaac* meant laughter. From the moment God gave Sarah and Abraham the promise of their son, Isaac, he'd planted a seed of laughter in their hearts. If Sarah had fully believed the Lord—who knows, she might have walked in genuine laughter from day one. Perhaps she didn't need to wait all those years for it.

So why did I hold back my laughter? Easy. Because whenever good things happened in my life, bad things seemed to follow. I'd learned to hope for the best and prepare for the worst.

Apparently, God wanted something different from me. He wanted me to swing open the gate of my heart to his hilarious ways and leap into the future with unashamed expectancy.

*Lord, I see it now. I've made worry my secret sidekick. Please retrain my brain. I want to freefall into your arms and stop looking for safety nets. I'm done with worry. It's stolen too much. I want to savor each brief moment of Josiah's childhood, and I want to make your goodness known.*

God gave me a chance to share about his goodness with a group of men and women from a local gathering at Substance Church. I'd never been nervous about public speaking. In fact, I rather thrived on it. But when it came to talking about Josiah, which God put on my heart to do, I felt on edge.

"It's almost like he dreams," I told them. "But he also hears from Jesus and angels when he's awake."

Their eyes looked kind and caring, so I kept going. "I'm going to share a song that Josiah wrote in March, but first, let's define one of the words he used. **Guffaw.** When I asked him what it meant, this is what he typed: **a happy laugh for calm effects, a famous, fun feel.** So here goes:

I tune to heaven each lustrous night
Remembering doves
Joy singing fascinating music
For tens of thousands
Jesus requires songs of praise
Passionately as a guffaw, saturate him with ten guffaws
Festive faith, gifted and abetted, fashioned and made
For a best king
Naturally get a genuine tear gate open
Name a good feel, undone bliss, a nifty guarantee
A gigantic noise of guffaws
For roses more than the eye can see
Reap tears for jars. Latter rains end your fears
Take my fun, gentle ways
Go name it now a non-issue
And see otters play for you."

I looked around the room. "Josiah's last line made me cry," I said, "He doesn't know this, but I *love* otters! I think they're funny and playful, and I think God wanted to show me how much he's into the details. He knows all about me, and he knows about you too."

Afterward, a girl in her twenties approached me. "My roommates and I have a weekly home gathering in Minneapolis with about eighteen or so people. We'd love to have you come share your story."

A few weeks later, we all crammed into her living room, and I shared what God taught me about Sarah and how I wanted to be able to laugh at the days to come. "Leave it to God," I said, "to work me over in the shower when I'm naked and vulnerable. I suppose it's the best place to flat-out ugly cry because you don't have to worry about your mascara crises."

At the end of our time together, I had a sweet opportunity to hear their hearts.

"I've had a lot of disappointments," said a slim girl with dark hair. "My mom has bad anxiety, and I think I picked it up because I'm always a little on edge."

I prayed for her, and another girl spoke up. "Sometimes I think God has something great for me, an exciting design or a destiny, but when nothing happens, I let my dreams die."

My heart went out to her. "It's hard to keep believing for your dreams," I said, "but the God who resurrected his Son has the power to resurrect each of the dreams he gave you."

The hostess, a sweet-faced girl with bobbed hair and a wide smile, thanked me for coming. "Tahni has really blessed us tonight. Let's gather around her and pray blessings over her family and ministry."

Tears filled my eyes as they prayed. I'd come to share and ended up receiving more than I gave. Didn't God always work that way in his kingdom?

I laughed as I drove back home. *God, I'd love to do more of this kind of thing. I want to be an encourager and spiritual mother to younger women. Thank you a thousand times over for using my pain to fuel my passion!*

# 15

# Healing

"Love fuels your healing."

– Josiah Cullen

*Summer 2013*

When Josiah and I arrived at the Giggle Factory in Hudson, Wisconsin, he froze in the doorway.

"Hey, what's wrong? Go in." I nudged him toward the second door to the indoor playground, but he acted like a bull in a cage. People shot us looks as they squeezed by. Kids usually wanted to stay longer, not the other way around.

Josiah had liked this place the last time, but something must have just triggered him. Perhaps the wild mix of kids' voices sent his brain into sensory overload. I knew he wanted to join the fun, but felt paralyzed. Well, I could keep pressing, but I decided to follow his cue and leave.

Josiah's resistance reminded me of the time we stopped at a Burger King, and he dropped in a heap in the play area. His screeches sounded like those of a wounded animal, and he refused to move. Scooping him up, I stumbled past the staring people on what felt like a ten-mile walk to the parking lot.

But I had other stories that topped that one. Like the time in the health food store when a male customer started yelling at me. "Would you shut that kid up? I can't take it anymore. You need to make him stop touching things. You never should have brought him here!"

"Sorry, he can't help it," I said, dashing out.

The clerk ran after me. "Ma'am, I'm so sorry he yelled at you. Please feel free to come back anytime."

These kinds of trials made me want to plunge deeper into God's Word and cozy up with him. So that's what I did when I returned home.

I read about the apostle Paul's battle with his flesh, and I thought about Josiah's uncooperative body along with my own internal wrestling.

"Although I want to do good, evil is right there with me. For in my inner being I delight in God's law; but I see another law at work in me, waging war against the law of my mind and making me a prisoner of the law of sin at work within me. What a wretched man I am! Who will rescue me from this body that is subject to death? Thanks be to God, who delivers me through Jesus Christ our Lord!" (Romans 7:21–25).

I loved Paul's answer to that depressing question. Jesus. I also appreciated how I could apply that to Josiah. No matter how enslaved an autistic child might feel in his uncooperative body, God longed to pour out his grace and victory. Something I loved to watch him do in our family.

I'd never formally asked the Lord to send Josiah a friend who would understand him, but he'd heard my heart anyway. Through Facebook, he led us to twelve-year-old Philip, Josiah's first pen pal.

**Dear Philip,**

**Both of us are peaceful when we can communicate. I like music that is melodic. Like I sense my soul turning portions of my soul yipping to soul sipping. I kiss heaven with my songs to luminate Jesus' love. I am pint-sized outside, but I am big inside, like you are, Philip.**

**Songs I sing are not with my mouth yet, but I will sing with**

my mouth soon. I take that as an attention getter for you, Philip, since rotely, we dominantly don't use our mouths. But I tell you that I will use my mouth, and you will too! Our words will flow.

Worth is not what you do, but it is bondage not to show what you know. It is like the answer is totally blowing my mind. It is like a most excellent picture of notes of music on my head, because I know that now, Philip!

Healing comes with simple truths, would you agree? It's like I am pictured in a new light in my mind. I am prized because I am worthy, period. My voice is like a cold, motionless corpse, but I feel it positioning to speak. Could it come with boy's picture of worthiness?

Your nets are piled high with wonder because of your photography. Photos, truly tangible timed photos, are tremendous fun to luminate especially when pondering creation.

I hear that school starts soon for you, Philip. It is Philip that works hard to wear the much-loved badge of "trout" on his sash, because trout swim upstream, Philip. Way to go! Slim pickings, Lord knows, to find a good trout like you, Philip, that will swim for miles upstream.

Do you have a pet? I have a dog named Lucy. It is so fun to have a dog, Philip!

It is more than expected to have a friend now. It is so precious to me, Philip. Sometimes I feel alone. It's so much sadder when you don't have a friend.

We should meet someday,
Josiah

Like Josiah, Philip had been through RPM training and knew how to touch people's hearts. Josiah beamed when I read him Philip's words:

*I am attracted to certain things like leaves and flowers. I am drawn to their beauty. Part of me wants to be kind to nature, but my impulsive mind wants to pick the flowers and twirl them in my* hands. *I can't seem to stop myself. I see the flowers and I know I shouldn't pick them, but my hands have a mind of their own. I feel bad.*

*My mom has to remind me over and over not to pick the flowers. I can attack my impulse when someone can stop me with a word, but a mean tone makes me want to do it more. Mean manners toward me hurt my feelings.*

*I am lacking impulse control to make my body obey my brain. It is frustrating. I am like an amputee with phantom limbs. I seem to have limbs, but I can't feel mine. I have to see them to know they are there.*

*I can feel them better when I move. My body doesn't feel like it belongs to me, but my mind is mine. I am making an effort to make my body more obedient by meaningful activities like chores and bike riding.*

*No person should meaninglessly live life. They should find their talent and master it. My message to parents is give us opportunities to practice our movements in a purposeful way. Help us make plans to use lots of muscle memory by going to the trouble of teaching hobbies and useful skills.*

*Please be patient with us. I am managing my body as best as I can. No one wants to be a nuisance.*

*From, Philip*

Just as God connected Philip and Josiah, he led me to Sue Rampi, a wise older woman who had heard about me after I spoke at Substance Church. When Sue asked if she could treat me to lunch, I readily agreed. We ate Chinese at P.F. Chang's, and I felt an instant connection.

"I hear you nailed it and left everybody encouraged," she said. "I would have been there if I hadn't been on a mission trip."

"Oh, thanks," I said. "My friend Michele told me great things about you and your family's ministry."

"Likewise. And that son of yours, Josiah. He sounds like quite the guy."

I chuckled. "Yeah, that's one way to describe him."

Sue and I exchanged stories. She reminded me of Acts 2:17: "In the last days, God says, I will pour out my Spirit on all people. Your sons and daughters will prophesy, your young men will see visions, your old men will dream dreams."

Sue leaned in. "I have a strong sense that Josiah is going to be used by God in a huge way. God handpicked him and set him apart."

Something leaped in me with her words. "You're dialed into these kinds of things, aren't you?"

She nodded. "When I was little, I could see into the spiritual realm. Angels, demons, the whole deal. I had all kinds of experiences I didn't know what to do with, and I didn't have the guts to talk about them. Not like your speechless son."

I sipped my water. "I love hearing about this. I desperately want to understand what Josiah's encountering so I can parent him better. I think we'll have lots to talk about. Michele told me you're like a spiritual mother to many and that you've been in ministry for decades."

"Forty years. I've traveled across the world, and I've seen all kinds of miracles. Blind eyes open, deaf ears hearing. Especially in places like Honduras."

"Wow. That must be so gratifying. Why do you think we don't see as much of that in America?"

She stabbed a piece of broccoli. "I don't know. Maybe people need to be more desperate for God."

"I'm desperate," I said. "Joe recently found a video of Josiah when he was fifteen months old, before he had autism. I'm telling you, his face shone, he was so full of life. For the longest time, I wouldn't even look at any old pictures of him."

"In that case," she said, "it must have been hard for you to watch the video."

"Yeah, but it was worth it. Josiah kept looking at himself in the big mirror at the Children's Museum. Boy, he sure enjoyed seeing his twinkly eyes and mischievous grins. He'd look at the camera, giggle, and give little squeals. What a ham. He used to be so over-the-top sociable."

She handed me a Kleenex. "Did you let him watch the video?"

I nodded. "He watched it over and over, completely mesmerized and tickled. Oh, and then he wrote about it. Would you like to see what he said?" I reached into my bag and pulled out the iPad. "This is the beauty of his writing it down. It's all recorded."

**I love seeing myself without tics sponsored by autism. It's a tremendous feeling to know tics are not me. Duh, but it is like doubt was leading me to believe closing the door naturally meant losing me.**

**It's a different view with this mirror. I see me, not autism. A poet, yes. A worship leader, yes. Autism, no. Pray for speech. It probes me to hit and claw when I actually ideally want healing so much.**

"Wow, that boy knows who he is and what he wants."

I shrugged. "I don't know if he sees himself as a worship leader in heaven or on earth. If he means on earth … well, that would certainly take a huge miracle."

"God can do it, Tahni."

"Yes he can. He recently allowed me to meet a lady who'd been healed of high-functioning autism."

"High-functioning or low," she said, "God is greater." She pushed our empty plates out of the way and grabbed my hands. "I want to stand in agreement with you for Josiah's healing. In Jesus' name, that boy will talk!"

Goosebumps trickled down my arms as she poured her heart out to God on my behalf. An hour ago I hadn't even known this woman, but God used her to give me an extra jolt of faith.

*God, you wouldn't tease me about all these great things you want to do. You wouldn't set up a divine appointment only to set me up for more disappointment—would you?*

# 16

# Old Friendships

"Be the space the Spirit needs to reach this place."

– Josiah Cullen

**Summer 2013**

Of all the therapists Josiah worked with at Partners, we'd never forgotten Kim, his favorite. What a treat to hear from her when she started following *Josiah's Fire* on Facebook.

*Hi Tahni! Now that Josiah has been communicating with you, I was wondering if you could ask him if he remembers me. Please tell him that I am so proud of him, and it fills me with joy that he has found his voice. There is not a word I read from him that I am not in awe and then nod my head, because I knew he had that philosopher in him.*

*Yes, Josiah! You will sing with the birds. You can do anything, inspire many, and have found your blue jay communication! You are the boy that changed my life, and I am forever grateful. I celebrate with you all! I hope everything else is going well for your family.*

*Many blessings and big laughing hugs,*

*Kim*

I knew I had to talk to Josiah about this, so I wandered into his room. "Hey, JoJo. You used to have a therapist named Kim. You probably don't remember her much because you were only four when she left Partners, but you really impacted her life. After she worked with you, she went back to school to get her masters. She wants to work with gifted children and do family counseling. How about I read you what she wrote?"

He played Family Playhouse on his iPad while I shared Kim's message. Then he scooted beside me to pound out a reply.

**Absent, fun Kim. Need gem's fabulous peace. Gem laughed and God sang.**

**Gem gallops with men who ten times pester numb lungs. Best gone nemesis is Matthew. Gem's beast of a beast's fast friend hit a beam on her fast heart.**

**God is not feeling himself near, not because demons cease your hidden gem angel, but because bad demon is bringing fear to same near gem. Jesus fanned a flame for a beacon to help you.**

**Best boy still remembers fun best girl. I can baffle fun gem because I go near your gabby angel, ceasing bad demon of Gemini. Jesus lavishes his fanned flame of love.**

**Get God, Kim, for your leg fails to stand without him. Name it demon's last day. Angel of fun peace will fabulously fall on you.**

I drew back. "Um … I'm supposed to send her this?"

"Eee," he squealed.

*Oh Lord, you're going to have to help me here.*

I wrote an introduction to add to Josiah's message.

*Hi Kim.*

*I showed Josiah a picture of you when you had long hair, then read him your note and asked if he remembered you. Below is what came out next.*

*I must tell you, since you are one who is tuned into spiritual things, that his understanding can only be described as supernatural.*

*It all shifted in September. Josiah started typing, and I've discovered that he somehow visits heaven and "sees" into the spirit. He prophesies and is crazy hooked up and connected to God. I never taught him the things he comes out with. He writes with a language, cadence, and intelligence all his own.*

*I hope you don't regret me asking him about you now. But it* sounds like there are some warnings and also reminders that heaven is looking out for you. He also seems to know and remember you in an astounding soul connection kind of way.

Can you please let me know if this resonates and is accurate? Some of the things he writes are a mix of past, present, and future. If you have any questions, please ask. I often ask him for more explanations too.

He uses the word "gem" a lot. When he says that, he's referring to you—a person heaven sees as a gem. You're loved.

Kim responded later that night:

Tahni! This is incredible! I keep reading it.

I completely believe and feel that he truly connects to God.

You are correct. It is a mix of past, present, and a little bit of future. I believe this is a message for me and also to demonstrate God's connection for you. I have gone sentence by sentence. I believe I understand most of it, but of course there are still interpretations and questions with some of the symbolism—especially the future part. I am assuming I will find more meaning later.

I have recently been on a spiritual journey, finding and making connections to the spiritual world. I hope I don't sound loony to you. I feel comfortable in sharing with you, understanding that you have a caring open heart and would not make a negative judgment—also it will lessen your worry about the message.

I moved to Denver to begin a journey of understanding myself and separating myself from a community that wasn't helping when it came to working through some of my personal issues (comes with the territory of being a "hippie," I guess :)). I have fought for my happiness, and believe that with my counseling field I'm finally finding it.

I believe this is the demon Josiah references. My tarot card readings consistently mention how past traps block me from connecting spiritually ... I get many signs to increase the power in my choices.

*Matt is my ex-boyfriend who I thought was my love, and I
moved in with. Once I moved to the mountains with him, it revealed
his addiction and I experienced a lot of emotional abuse. He chose
substances, I chose health. My choice and strength to get out of the
relationship and restart my life led me to begin the spiritual healing
I am currently on.*

*I am completely over this whole dating thing and am just ready
to find my soul mate. I am currently dating a Gemini. I think Josiah
is referencing that he is not my soul mate, that I will be sad to know
that, however there will be a conversation and lessons that will bring
me closer to understanding myself.*

*I give a lot of energy to my partners, but that also takes a toll
on my energy/light. I believe he is talking about my healing process,
finding my spirituality and personal strength and not letting fear
hold me back. My current lessons revolve around independence and
confidence.*

She went on to explain about her upcoming trip to Ecuador,
but I was stuck on her reference to her ex-boyfriend. For Pete's
sake, Josiah had known his name!

The next morning, I strolled into Josiah's room and watched
him whack his bed with his toy lizard. "Hey, buddy. Good to see
you." I gave him a hug. "Kim wrote you back, and I'd love to hear
what you think of her interpretation."

He clicked his tongue as I read it to him.

I stroked his cheek. "Well, what do you think?"

His finger tapped like crazy.

**Bad interpretation, Kim. Your near angel is real. Lad is calmly
warning you. Let Jesus lead a genuine restoration.**

**The demon Gemini is not your new boyfriend. It is a bad
demon, literally. Gem, cap your mental gate. Your nemesis longs
to net you. I see it near you. Make Neptune take a hike and tune
into God, not the nature feast about to happen.**

**Kim, faith is fun. Dance before him, not the ABCs killing**

**your passion. Worship Jesus, Kim. Worship joyfully. Worship expressively. Worship richly. Worship jets you to his power. It is power over the woes that poach your sleep. It is perfect peace in Jesus, not Satan's mental totems.**

**Picture it done. Satan is ruining angel's dashing peace to your tan body. Let me lessen your demon gears to famous worship God's way.**

**The angel talked to you this Monday last and fanned a flame. Tell gem Kim I can feel her spirit near me. Family friend, I labor nearly because I love you.**

"What are you getting us into, buddy? And what do you mean about the ABCs?"

**The burdens of cares.**

*Help me, Jesus. I have a few of those right now.* I grabbed the laptop and hurried outside to the lawn chair.

*Hi Kim! You're right, I don't judge. My job is to always love and bless. I read your message to Josiah and asked something like, "How did she do with the interpretation?"*

*I need to tell you that Josiah went for a passionate no-holds redirection. Believe me, I understand these words hit at the very core of everything you hold close and true.*

*As you go on your trip, I have a feeling things will get clearer. I have never talked about any other religious or spiritual practices to Josiah, so none of this comes from his natural environment.*

*Feel free to ask more questions to Josiah for clarification. Blessings on your trip and on your journey! You are 100 percent loved.*

Kim responded:

*Wild. Okay, I will take him more literally. I do believe that there is value and a connection within all views, experiences, teachings, and lessons.*

A couple weeks later, I heard from her again.

*My trip is wonderful. In fact, I have indeed been experiencing a few moments of God and messages. I am happy to recognize them and feel that I see them more because of Josiah's message.*

"Hey, look, Josiah. Kim wrote you back." I read it aloud to him and drank in his reply.

**Kim, you sowed more positive seeds. You still question God's good intentions toward you. Ponder God. Tonight's stunning nest toasts to most wonderful Kim. A student of God fondles obedient magnificent pleasures; mundane idols ponder nutty works.**

**Your muse gets pockets of faith, but longs for, quote me, love, not pondering of Jesus. Model near-mute boy. I get a beautiful purpose. Genuinely voice of mute will fend for the state of pent-up kids. Picture it done.**

Oh, mercy. His boldness. Where did he get it? Certainly not from me. And how strange to see him use the word *mute* again, when none of us even used that term. Sheesh, if I had my way, I'd keep his message from Kim, but how could I do that when Josiah only wanted to help in her spiritual search?

*Father, thank you that perfect love casts out all fear. Please help me love like you love—with a love that's bigger than self-consciousness. These words sound dangerous to me, but I know you will use them for good. Knowing you love me, I give you permission to use me however you choose. I'm yours.*

Joe and I started dating after performing in a college play. Little did we know how dramatic our lives would become.

Daddy gave his little girl away to be married. Sadly, he died of a heart attack just a little more than a year later.

Our son was born on October 4, 2005, and we gave him the name Josiah, which means "fire of the Lord."

Grandpa and Grandma Cullen loved on their new grandson.

At eight-months-old, Josiah was happy, healthy, and bursting with life. He had no sensory issues. Zero. Zilch.

He took in all his surroundings on his first birthday—especially the cake!

Josiah interacted like a typical fourteen-month-old. He looked at the camera and pretended to play on the phone. If only things hadn't changed.

When Josiah was eighteen months old, Joe's parents noticed how intently he gazed at fence patterns; so later they brought up the topic of autism.

It wasn't long before Josiah slipped away some-where else. He completely stopped looking at us and responding to his name.

By the time he was two, he had no spark left in his eyes.

At three, full-time therapy didn't help as much as everybody hoped.

What's this? Four-year-old Josiah discovered his dad's iPod with interest.

When I heard about a new invention called the iPad, I preordered one and received it on April 3, 2010.

The new iPad helped Josiah communicate basic requests with his therapists.

The iPad came with a new addition to our family: our Maltipoo pup, Lucy.

When Josiah was introduced to a communication method called the Rapid Prompting Method (RPM), it opened a whole new door for us.

I practiced RPM with Josiah 20–25 minutes at a time; and let's just say, he wasn't always the most agreeable student.

In the fall of 2012, seven-year-old Josiah experienced a shocking communication breakthrough on the iPad. And I began to take it everywhere so he could type his thoughts and wishes.

Introducing Josiah's iPad with the iMean alphabetical letterboard app.

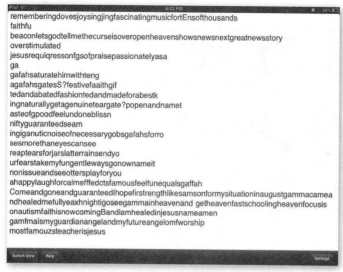

iPad ᵍ 8:03 PM ● 36%

rememberingdovesjoysingjingfascinatingmusicfortEnsofthousands
faithfu
beaconletsgodtellmethecurseisoveropenheavenshowsnewsnextgreatnewsstory
overstimulated
jesusrequiqressonfgsofpraisepassionatelyasa
ga
gafahsaturatehimwithteng
agafahsgatesS?festivefaaithgif
tedandabatedfashiontedandmadeforabestk
ingnaturallygetagenuineteargate?popenandnamet
asteofgpoodfeelundoneblissn
niftyguaranteedseam
ingiganuticnoiseofnecessarygobsgafahsforro
sesmorethaneyescansee
reaptearsforjarslatterrainsendyo
urfearstakemyfungentlewaysgonownameit
nonissueandseeottersplayforyou
ahappylaughforcalmefffedctsfamousfeelfunequalsgaffah
Comeandgoneandguaranteedlhopefirststrengthlikesamsonformysituationinaugustgammacamea
ndhealedmefullyeaxhnightigoseegammainheavenand gethavenfastschoolingheavenfocusis
onautismfaithisnowcomingBandiamhealedinjesusnameamen
gamfmaismyguardianangelandmyfutureangelomfworship
mostfamouzsteacherisjesus

Switch View   Help                                                    Settings

I saved all his writings. Too bad they didn't have any spaces and punctuation.

Each week in the summer I took Josiah out of therapy for special mother-son outings, which he called "Feminine Mondays."

Joe took Josiah to his first major league ballgame, a daddy's dream come true.

Joe joined Josiah at a sensory-friendly performance of Beauty and the Beast, and afterward Josiah wrote several pages describing its significant spiritual parallels.

Kudos to the lady who helped me hold it together through all the crazy twists and turns in our autism world. I love you, Mom!

Mom and a couple friends joined me when God directed me through Josiah to pray over our city from its highest point, the Minneapolis Witch's Hat Tower.

While at a family reunion, Josiah wrote the most tender touching words to my cousin Talitha and presented them to her with tears in his eyes.

At the Irish Fair, where Josiah and I had some interesting encounters.

After Josiah's words greatly impacted artist Scott Sample, he gave us one of his paintings. We hung it over our couch where Josiah continues to share God-glorifying insights from heaven.

## 17

# Limitless Love

"Meet Father as a holder of love, and you will get love.
Might Papa God be generous to a fault in these hours?
Might his joy be very full?"

– Josiah Cullen

**Take me to the Mall of America and God will show you something that surprises you.**

"Surprises me?" I shifted on the chilly zoo bench. "Well, that's a big thought ... but I'm game. Let's do it."

Josiah tugged me to the car.

"Wait. Slow down." Goodness, talk about a bundle of energy. I buckled him in his booster seat, and away we went. Most kids would be pooped after an action-packed day with the animals, but not Josiah. Each activity only seemed to rev him up more.

I thought of how he'd dragged his hands against the walls in the Tropical Zone, as if reading Braille. The birds and monkeys made their noises, and Josiah made his. When he saw the stingrays, he plunged his hands into the water to pet their slimy bodies.

During the 3D IMAX movie about Kenya, his eyebrows shot up and down and so did his butt. He hopped back and forth from his seat to my lap like he couldn't decide which was more comfortable. But we were watching a public movie—something we never used to be able to do!

When the credits went up, I'd asked him, "What part did you like best?" I thought he'd say something about the lions, leopards, wildebeests, or inspiring young men who braved the African landscape. Instead he typed about how much he liked watching the girls have a jumping contest.

"What did you like about it?" I said.

**Mom, shouldn't we all be willing to give big joyful jumps, higher and higher for God?**

Of course. Why hadn't I thought of that?

I helped him out of the car and into the mall's parking garage. Instinctively, I squeezed his hand so he wouldn't jet off. The automatic doors opened and we stepped inside, instantly bombarded by clusters of people. They reminded me of fish swimming every which way, looking for something, who knows what.

I used to shy away from big places with Josiah, especially malls, because if I couldn't make a fast getaway, forget it. I'd faced far too many meltdowns where I had to carry a screaming, kicking kid to the car.

This year, however, when the Mall of America hosted the Autism Speaks walkathon, Josiah experienced a turnaround and started liking it. You'd think the overstimulation would get to him, but somehow the constant buzz of activity had a calming effect. Smaller places, on the other hand, made it too easy for him to hyper-focus on the sights and sounds. They screeched into his senses like unwelcome guests, wreaking havoc on all of us.

"JoJo, what do you say we grab a bite to eat and beat the five o'clock rush?"

I steered him into line, and five seconds later he started acting up.

"Josiah, what are you doing?" He leaned over the divider rope and bent back and forth like a monkey, while heat crawled up my face. "Stop!" He didn't listen. I wedged myself between him and the rope and tried to block him from his gymnastics. Too bad I couldn't block people's stares.

As soon as they handed me Josiah's food, I grabbed his hand and hustled us over to Noodles & Company to buy me a salad. "Over here, Josiah." We opted for the quieter section, and I made small talk while he gobbled his bunless burger and ice cream. After he finished, I had a fairly good idea where he'd want to go next. To a place he could find blindfolded: the toy store.

As I tromped beside him, we passed the amusement park with its screaming kids, but Josiah wasn't interested. He pressed ahead at an even pace. Then something came over him. He switched into high gear like a dog chasing a squirrel.

"Josiah, wait! This isn't the way to the toy store." Goodness, he'd gotten so big I could hardly control him. "Josiah, please." I tightened my grip, trying to slow him, but he didn't stop until he took me to a bench in front of a glass rail. There, he plopped us both down. Okay, now what? I glanced through the glass at the stores and floors below and at the window in front of me with its home décor.

"What's the deal, Josiah?" I pulled out his iPad and watched his finger go wild.

**Hobnob with that nice girl placing little stares now my way, spiritually working to voice little durable words to voice for doubters.**

"Girl? What girl? Josiah, we're at a mall. There are tons of girls. What are you talking about?"

**Love is love. Tell her that. I'll be forced to voice my love for her myself. Now is the time to work the floor like it is party time. Tell her words. Take her breath away. Tell her that love is born out of choosing God, not choosing Wicca.**

**Hope is love, not more daddy issues. Pick a spiritual daddy. It is boy's father; it is God. Choose him, not a brotherhood of robbers. Because "you need me," God says.**

My heart raced. *Oh God, please don't tell me you want me to walk up to a stranger, a witch stranger, and tell her this ... word from heaven. Can't we just go back to McDonald's, so he can act like a monkey?*

I glanced left and right, trying to find this possible witch. It wasn't like he could even point her out. No, he had to go and leave me in silence.

Just then, I noticed a group of young people in their early twenties at the other end of the curved glass rail. Could Josiah be referring to one of those girls? They looked serious as they talked to one of the guys. Wait. The girl leaning against the glass wore a long black cape.

*Why, Lord? Isn't my life crazy enough? I feel like an elastic band about to break. You don't really want me to do this, do you? Why didn't you just let us go home after the zoo and take a nap like normal people?*

"Ahh…" Josiah groaned.

"JoJo, are you trying to tell me I'm supposed to walk up to a group of complete strangers and deliver this message to a Wiccan girl?"

His answer sped up my heart.

**Yes.**

"But it might not even mean anything to her."

**You need to tell her.**

"Seriously, Josiah. I don't even know which girl you mean. You need to describe her first."

But just then, the whole group started toward us. If I didn't catch them now, they'd walk by and I'd miss my opportunity. I took a deep breath and, ignoring all sound reasoning, I jumped to my feet and waved. "Excuse me."

They turned. The girl in the black cape squared back her shoulders and blinked. Her dark auburn hair sat loosely on her shoulders, and her long legs in fishnet hose poked out the front of her dress.

Clearing my throat, I managed a smile. "Hi, sorry to bother you. Do you have a second? I have a question if you don't mind."

She put a hand on her hip. "Sure, what is it?"

I shifted. "By any chance, are you at all spiritually inclined?"

She glanced at her friends. "Yeah, I suppose you could say that."

"Um, my name is Tahni, and the reason I'm asking is because my son Josiah here is like that too. He has autism, and he's nonverbal, but he communicates by typing on his iPad." I held out the screen with one hand and Josiah with the other. "Sorry, it's hard to read. Josiah doesn't use spaces, so it's like a big run-on sentence. I stopped you because Josiah just wrote a message, and I think it might be for you. Do you mind if I read it?"

"Sure, I guess."

I drew in a breath, read her the whole thing, and searched her eyes. "Did it mean anything to you?"

"Uh, not really…"

*Great*, I thought. *So much for that idea.*

Just then, the bright-blond girl with the bob spoke up. "That message isn't about her. It's about me." She peeled back the shoulder of her shirt to reveal a tattoo of a five-point star inside a circle, a pentagram. "*I'm* in Wicca," she said. "They tell me that *I* have daddy issues. The whole time you were reading, I felt hot. That thing's talking about *me*."

Air returned to my lungs as I glanced at the girl in the cape. "Sorry for the misunderstanding. Your outfit threw me off." Feeling foolish, I forced myself to focus on the blond girl. "Okay, now that I've read you this, do you have any idea what it means?"

One of her male friends spoke up. "Sam, I think it means you're not supposed to be in Wicca anymore."

"This is freaking me out a little," I admitted. "I mean, how could this happen? We're standing in the biggest mall in America and the God of the universe, the Christian God, managed to intersect our paths at just the right moment to give you this message. Sam, what do you think about that?"

"I'm really not sure what to think," she said. "I believe in a higher power, but I don't really believe in God the way you do. I used to be Lutheran, but I haven't gone to church since ninth grade. Man, this is weird. I really don't know what to do with this."

"Well, you know what I think?" I said. "I think it's amazing that somebody up there would want to give you this message so much that he used a mom and her little autistic boy who knew nothing about you."

"I know," she said. "I don't know what to say."

"That's okay. It's a lot to process. Would it be possible to have your e-mail address? I'd love to send you the message so you can read it later."

"Sure." She jotted it down.

"Thanks." I turned to the others with open arms. "Hey, I'm glad I met you guys. Thanks for being so patient with me."

My heart beat wildly, even after we said goodbye. I knew what I wanted to do next. I sat back on the bench with Josiah. "Now I want you to tell me, what just happened there?"

But he didn't answer. Instead he wrote another message for Sam.

**Obey me, not holy Wicca or little orders of demons that mock you sickly with real spit on your face. I am the God of the most informative cosmos pointing you out. The vote is in. I am docked, but I am coding party girl with open revelation, troubling her now.**

**Trouble is that you are truly questioning everything, but my work tells you that roses demonstrate my love. My work is yet to be stirred. It is pictures to your mind. It is worship to your words. Pick, pick, pick, Sam. The holy one picks you. Most high Jehovah God is my name. Poetry will double when you choose me, not Wicca, not named and unnamed gods that are demons.**

**Jesus is the most hope you will ever find. Could he be far, or could he be as close as, "Oh my God!" Language is most unusual to me. I am struggling with this candescent Papa who packs this little punch in my spirit! I am forced to hold my hands up to heaven and say, "I choose God! I choose Jesus! I choose Daddy! I choose boy's papa. I choose daughter! I choose yeses that pick me because I am worth so much to God that I am eager to have life again!"**

**Dine on that, Sam. Vote is in my work to love you like a daughter. Pick me to forge a new path of mimicking the boy's Lord, not the witches' lord.**

All the way home, Sam's face blinked back at me. When I flopped on my downstairs sectional, I decided to preface Josiah's words with a few of my own.

*Dear Sam,*

*I'm glad I got your e-mail address! Just one favor: please keep an open mind and heart as you read this. Think open, not closed, and see if something doesn't get confirmed in your spirit that this is true and is for YOU. Surely you must already know I have absolutely no motive here, except to deliver a note that tells you that you are loved. That's it. If you want to ask questions or discuss this further, it's totally up to you. I'm happy to do whatever I can.*

I copied and pasted everything together. Boy, if Sam would allow God to break through the walls of her mind, she'd see how God loves her beyond the capability of any earthly father. God eagerly desired this love relationship with her—but did she? I so prayed she would. Then I pressed *send.*

Whether or not Sam ever changed, I knew I sure had. I'd always known that God doesn't play favorites, he loved us all the same, but now I *really* knew it. It wasn't a matter of "us" and "them." God didn't hold people of other religions at an arm's length and call the rest of us close. He just didn't. No matter how far we strayed, he'd never stop trying to bring us back to himself—even in the biggest mall in America.

*Okay, Daddy. I guess you weren't kidding when you said you had a surprise for me at the mall today. Thanks for giving me strength to step into this new way of thinking. And please increase my bravery—in case there's ever a next time.*

# 18

# New Classroom

"I give you a loan of making you see;
poor in spirit is not poor in me."
– Josiah Cullen

*Summer 2013*

I rubbed Josiah's back as he shoveled in his vanilla ice cream. "This is huge," I told him. "Once the summer's over, we're going to transition you from Partners into an autism class in a public school."

His tongue batted his lips for stray ice cream as I grabbed a cloth to take care of the rest. "To smooth your transition, I'll be taking you out of Partners for the rest of the Mondays this summer. That will give us a bunch of extra-long weekends together. Won't that be great?"

He responded with two simple words: **feminine Mondays**.

I laughed. "Great name. I love it."

Over the next few months, I took him to parks, museums, quaint little towns, and artsy spots like the Franconia Sculpture Park. I laughed as he climbed their larger-than-life sculptures.

"What do you like about this place?" I asked.

**I like it because I can climb mountains to feel that best questions are answered and ponder baffling dealings.**

Before we left for a park one Monday, he expressed a unique wish: **let me listen to country music today, and it will tell me nutty truths about men's hearts.**

What? How strange. Joe and I didn't even listen to country music. To humor him though, I played country radio stations as we drove.

When we arrived, we discovered the park had been invaded by Girl Scouts and party inflatables. Oh no. They had a bouncy house. I barely had time to think before Josiah made a run for it.

"Hey, wait! We need to see if it's okay." I chased after him all the way over and breathlessly asked the lady, "Can I pay for this?"

"No, sorry. Insurance only covers kids from the camp."

"Josiah, wait!" But it was too late. He had already taken off his shoes and bounced in with the girls.

I broke into a sweat as the kids and adults watched me wedge my body through the narrow opening. Teetering back and forth, I clawed for my son, who always ended up just inches away from my grasp. Feminine Monday—yeah, right.

"Josiah, get over here. That's enough. Stop!" He hit and kicked while I lunged and grabbed. When I finally got him out, he ripped off his glasses and threw them on the pavement.

"Great. Now look what you've done. You scratched up your good lenses."

I drove away in tears, feeling defeated.

*God, this is too hard.*

Ten minutes later, I saw a private nature spot and pulled over for a bench break. "What happened, JoJo?"

There, under a poplar tree, my son wrote his first country song.

**Poor Man's Gospel**

**Kiss me, Jesus, please**
**I won't charge you any fees**

Telephone is a game man plays
Resist foolish man's ways
Quote me now, quote me then
Reason lends a silly den
Rise to the cream of the crop
Roses are buds pending a pop
Poor man's work is best forgotten
It is rotten, rotten, rotten
Hear me now, believe me later
Swearing tends to make a crater
Kiss me, Jesus, tears are rollin'
Kiss me now, peace is flowin'

Lots of people will see it, he added.

When summer drew to an end, Joe and I took Josiah for the mandatory psychological testing required for school. With so much going on, I'd been feeling conflicted lately. I still couldn't get the Partners therapists' words out of my head: *We hate to see Josiah leave, but he's probably gleaned as much out of ABA therapy as he's going to get … He has a tough time focusing on tasks, and he mostly looks bored and dialed out … It's time for him to have a new challenge.*

How strange that after six years and forty hours a week at the same place, it was time to move on.

I opened the door to the psychologist's office. "Be on your best behavior," I reminded him.

So what did he do after he stepped in? He took a great big elegant leap into the trash can.

The psychologist adjusted his glasses. "Why don't we move to the room next door?"

"Can you sort these colors?" he asked. I cringed when he took a seat across from Josiah, because Josiah always preferred to be side by side. "Focus," he said, squeezing a squeaky frog.

Josiah grunted, hardly poking at the spiral notebook of patterns.

Instead he hid behind my chair. Resorting to Plan B, the psychologist began to blow bubbles, which Josiah dutifully clapped with his hands.

"Maybe we should let him share his thoughts," Joe offered. "Josiah, tell Mom what's wrong."

I pulled out my iPad and held it while Josiah's finger moved painfully slow. "Keep going," I said. Then I showed his words to Joe.

**Stupid kid questions from man. I want to leave.**

Joe and I looked at the psychologist and suppressed a laugh.

"Phew," I said as we closed our car door. Then Joe and I burst into laughter. "Well, he didn't exactly cooperate with the testing, but at least we don't have to wonder what he thinks about it. Hey, can you imagine what might have happened if we told the psychologist everything?"

Joe chuckled. "'Well, you see, our son is hearing voices and experiencing heavenly encounters with angels.' Yeah, they'd probably come up with a whole brand-new label for him."

"Yeah," I said. "Or for me."

I turned and smiled at Josiah, our Mr. Amazing. Lately, I'd been affirming him with lines from the movie *The Help*, so I repeated those life-giving words aloud. "Josiah, *you are smart, you are kind, you are important.* Oh, and you are 100 percent loved."

A week before school, as I stirred a pot of stew, I watched Joe put his arm around Josiah on the couch.

"I know how you feel, JoJo," he said. "When I was nine, just a year older than you, my family moved from New York to North Dakota. I didn't know if I'd fit in at school either. Then, after a week, I really started to like it. Hey, I've got an idea. Why don't the two of us pick out some clothes for your big first day? Then after supper I'll take you to Walmart and we'll buy you a backpack."

Joe snapped a photo. He'd been documenting this big coming-of-age season, and my mama heart swelled with joy.

After supper, the three of us huddled on the couch to check out the school's preparation kit.

"Here's a picture of your new school," I said. "Look at those friendly looking aides."

"What's on your mind, buddy?" Joe asked.

Josiah looked tired as he typed. **I hope I don't hide in my sardine can. Sardines are known for their little cans, but much limits their motion in those cans. Delve into the ocean to see how they really live. They are so free and silver.**

**Destiny is trialed by trials, but hold your formation to be unified to resist the nets of so many fishermen trying to capture your present freedom.**

Josiah did fairly well on his first day, but according to the teacher, as soon as he walked inside, he decided to bypass the classroom and hightail it to the swings. This didn't surprise me, of course. At Partners they started their day with swings.

For some reason, sitting in a semi-circle with the other kids didn't appeal to Josiah. Instead he dashed off to squeeze his body into the windowsill.

As he sat with me, he shared snippets of how he felt misunderstood and how others couldn't quite grasp that he had a brain.

Unable to take this anymore, I set up an appointment with his occupational therapist and speech therapist. It was time to show them how he wrote with me on the iPad.

Their focused eyes quickened my heart as I supported Josiah's arm. This was it. I hoped and prayed some good would come of this, and that maybe they'd even be able to help Josiah with his computer keyboarding skills.

The occupational therapist broke the silence. "Wow. Very interesting. Look how calm he is with you. He won't sit still like that for us. We're seeing a whole different side of him."

"Oh, he can be up and down with me too," I admitted. "You guys might want to watch *A Mother's Courage*. It will help you learn more about the Rapid Prompting Method, the technique that started this whole thing."

But from the casual look in their eyes, I could tell they would never venture to manage him the same way. I refused to let it get to me though. Then Josiah's special education teacher started giving him thought-provoking questions to take home, and I had something new to be thankful for.

One day she sent us a note saying she wanted to share one of Josiah's essays with the kids in a regular classroom, and I could hardly wait to hear how it went.

According to the teacher's aide, Josiah had stood at her side in front of the class while she gave a dramatic reading on his persuasive argument about swings.

I imagined how conflicted Josiah must have felt, standing in that classroom when he wished he could be there all the time. In a class with typical kids who knew typical freedoms and lived typical lives.

It broke my heart when I found out he could only engage with the typical kids during music class or when he dropped off sharpened pencils for them. The haunting video from the autism conference came piercing back like an arrow: "We're doing great if we can teach them a few functional skills like crushing cans and shredding paper."

*Lord God, Josiah is as sharp as those pencils he sharpens. I beg you—in the midst of all his inner friction, pretty please keep him from breaking.*

## 19

# Open Heaven

"Courageous people sing even when tunes are silent.
They play the notes they hear in their heart."
– Josiah Cullen

Josiah and I cuddled up in my room under tented covers, clutching our iPads.

"What exactly happens when you have all those supernatural experiences?" I asked matter-of-factly. "Are you having dreams and visions? I'd really like you to help me understand how these kinds of things work."

He opened up like a human encyclopedia.

**An open vision is when I see something in front of my eyes like a reel, but it isn't yet happening. So I see it like it is going to happen, and I see it while I am awake. I see it with my spiritual eyes like full pictures. So I can hire it to be done in prayer. A closed vision is symbols or scenes that represent something else to understand it better. I see closed visions all the time in my mind.**

**A dream is a sleeping ordered to ring in truths only the spirit says to you without your studying it. So work it out to voice boundless dreaming, western church, because you are so stuck in logic. Trial this truth: God uses all of these to talk to us.**

**Hearing is when I hear something being said. It is like music to my inner ears, sounding out God's, Jesus', and angels' voices to**

then tell you. So that is hearing the voices tuned to the frequency of heaven to span the divide.

As much as I loved what he wrote, it almost overwhelmed me trying to grasp it.

"Please don't take this wrong, sweetheart, but how do you know you're not hallucinating or hearing things?"

Dent that idea. It's not inside of my mind, so it is not imagination or hallucination. Tragically, slanderous, troubling, faithless doctors might say otherwise, but oh well. So what?

Listening is my work, so when I can speak, I will show that I am saying clues totally by quoting my spiritual messengers, not myself, when I am slicing this place of the frequency of heaven.

Now, demons will try to trial this frequency sound as well, but, "pick a different channel, Satan, you don't belong there, so go away from this frequency. It is timed for my God's words, not yours."

I stared at his lit-up face, glowing from the iPad under the sheets, and I shivered. "Okay. How do you experience heaven? I mean, is it like a dream or a vision?"

I am taken up in the spirit to heaven. I am not awake, but it is not a dream because it is happening to me for real, like I am in my mind and in my spirit at the same time.

It seems like every night, I think. Angels come to take me. It's not always the same one. It makes a stirred-up sound, and we swoosh up through the clouds to nestle in mental feathers of the miraculous.

I land at a place of language. It is like everything is alive. Trees give ovations. Leaves sing. Fast, rich streets glow. Spanning fountains flow.

Rich outings make spellbound student voice, "Majestic is this place I'm seeing." For it is like days turn to weeks turn to years turn to decades in the one night staying in that place.

After I see what God wishes to show, I am transported back the same way so I can mark my sleep with dreams, to rest, and get up in peace most of the time.

**This is so precious to me, dear Mom. I am so excited to tell you what happens to me, so you are tasting my world more than before.**

Wow. I felt warm and shivery at the same time. To think that the God of the whole universe, who cuddled up with me and my son in our little home, was also inviting my son into his home. How? I mean, it wasn't like Josiah had died or had a near-death experience.

Ever since Josiah had broken the ice about heaven, it kept cropping up in his writings all over the place, especially in the middle of the night. Piece by piece, letter by letter, I watched it unfold, making earth appear drab in comparison.

**Heaven is holy. Gold is pure like glass, not solid but clear. Fountains go up into arcs and jump around like water is jumping and leaping into high air.**

**Huge mighty lakes of great crystals burst forth in colors mighty in every way. Ponds are jumbo there. Purple is greatly the purplest there. It is big to look on large nimble people, and not one is old or sick or lame there.**

I drew in his words like a rich fresh breath. "Oh, Josiah, what an incredible place. Tell me more."

**God shows me his name in his joy is Papa. He is nice in all possible ways. He shows me I'm his kid. Like I'm huge to him. I'm huge to him!**

**At his throne, it was big to hear him say, "I'm language of your paintings, of your harkening, of your poems, and of your songs. I'm language of your hoping and language of your justice."**

**It is all joy to hold my life in his hands. He shows me new ideas for justice. He tells me about kings and leaders of countries, and he shows me his plans for people in our lives. He is not just my Papa; he is everyone's Papa.**

My mind swirled to Josiah's recent words about detailed scientific solutions. One of them even involved autism. *Whoa,* I had said to myself. *What could this average mom do with all this?*

I passed it along to two trusted confidantes, who casually shared it with two doctor friends, who marveled at Josiah's biological insights, claiming that his scientific reasoning sounded viable and actually held potential.

Interestingly, when it came to Josiah describing his experiences in heaven, he refused to share everything. He told me God didn't want him to divulge certain parts.

"I can respect that." How could I not when he'd already shared so much? He'd unveiled so many mysteries, stretching my perspective.

**Hints are big in heaven, like bright lights shining toward rabbit holes that look so small. Stick your head in and they aren't small at all. You don't need very large hours to see more years than your days could ever count.**

One night, Josiah described going up in some kind of cable car. **This tramway is a tunnel that I am prized to go through. The stars were far beyond what you can imagine! I saw places like Mars and bantered with the angel all the way to heaven.**

**The angel was large and fast. He looked like an archangel but was not one of the top ones. He was kind. He blasted a trumpet. I arrived at the place of the Master's feet. Jesus' feet. He is amazing. For an hour I was thanked for my work on the earth like I was treasured from a king.**

Another night, Josiah shared how angels regularly took him to school in heaven. They ushered him to a building with no walls, and he interacted with other kids, some who were still alive on earth. I didn't understand it, but he described learning as "effortless and fun." Knowledge came as something "musically downloaded."

In one particular class of about fifty kids, Josiah sat at a triangular-shaped desk with two others. Sometimes Jesus taught them, but mostly his teachers consisted of the greats who learned notable lessons during their days on earth. After these people spoke, their angels would share their side of the story. That way the students received a full, balanced, spiritual, behind-the-scenes perspective.

One day, Abraham Lincoln taught Josiah's class. After Lincoln shared about his life, Abraham's angel explained how he stirred up Lincoln to feel conflicted, giving him the "muse" or "call to action." At that particular moment in time, Lincoln felt moved that slavery must stop, simply because Jesus died for the freedom of mankind. It started with an inner nudge. And with that, justice arose in Lincoln's mind.

**I was led by Abraham Lincoln and his angel to be spiritually aware of what happened on the other side of the veil that was earth's. Like the future will stir up the past. I saw it! Spiritual sparkles that will split the bonds of slavery over the black men and women to resist the lost blessing of freedom of America.**

Oh my word. What exactly had God opened up to me? What might all these incredible revelations do to our lives?

I sat on the edge of my seat as he shared about when Moses spoke in class.

**Moses tells me that standing on the rock, the angel lifted up his arms, not merely Aaron and Hur. Angels were keeping his doubts at bay. So it is with us today.**

**Class in heaven spans the most brilliant minds that ever lived. Mom, I am so rich now in my mysterious classroom that has a triangle desk to richly discuss three ideas. Not just one, but us working together as one to voice miracles, to voice faith again, to show how harkening to God would cause life to work so much better.**

He motored to the table and took a gulp of grape juice. My heart beat with excitement as I pulled him back to the couch to continue.

**I saw Renoir paint his leading canvas. I heard Bach sound it out with rich opuses to life in his care. Ordinary people shook the rafters like art was love and songs were joy.**

**Quite a sight to see the daily workers do what they did on**

earth. **Scientists, chemists, jovial carpenters, kings, riders, lofty rich ideas kissing their minds. They jousted the heavens all the time.**

**Picture this school in eternity. Jesus picks the subjects I get to learn.**

Are you kidding? Talk about a spiritual goldmine! I wanted to share this with everybody, but at the same time I didn't. It was enough to just keep up on Facebook with his regular down-to-earth truths, principles, and insights.

People commented on his writing style. A linguist dropped me a private message, insisting that in all her years in the field, she had never seen writing as unique as Josiah's. God was behind this. My heart felt so full of heaven I could burst.

One morning before breakfast, I asked Josiah if he could tell me more about the other two kids at his desk.

**Yes. Yes. Usually these two are at my table. They are also majorly alive in the earth. Landon is about my age, and his hair is light blond. Laura is artsy all the time, noting her big ideas in language of poetry. She is my age too, and bold enough to maybe be a girl with a mop of light red hair. Naturally she is a nice girl.**

I laughed. "What do you guys talk about?"

**Just little conversations all over our joy. We were chosen to learn in heaven to look on our major world and build our hope up in our Lord in the earth again.**

"What are you like in heaven?"

**I'm fully all right in every way. I talk. I sing. I walk. I run. I'm able to do everything, making all polite gains in every nimble way in heaven.**

"I'd love to hear about the other fifty students. What do they all have in common? Is there something special about them?"

**My class is motioned by God to learn holy abilities and base it on his way and not Lucifer's naughty ways.**

*Hold it together*, I told myself. "When you aren't at your desk," I said, "what else do you do when you're learning?"

**We go out. It is very big to look around in heaven, making big hellos to passerbys on little paths.**

**Have you ever met one holy man in your life who has built a huge temple? I have.**

**If God wants us to know about sound, his great roar makes a sound and we see it in major waves in our eyes. It is huge to see sound, Mom. Just go and touch sound.**

**This is my night in great learning by looking on how ideas work. History is looking from heaven's perspective and valuing bold people.**

"Speaking of history, JoJo, did I ever talk to you about Abraham Lincoln?"

**You read one note about his basics as president.**

"Okay," I said. "I'd forgotten about that. What did Lincoln look like?"

**He was young like twenty maybe. Each person wears a robe. No top hat or black suit. No beard. He just looks like Abraham Lincoln, Mom. It is just known. You just automatically know who people are up there.**

"Can you remember some other things about Lincoln from when you met him in heaven?"

**Yes. He was notable. Like he got a natural jury to point out the bold harm to judge a man by his skin color. He based his life on moving language to look on men as equal. This is big in the eyes of God.**

"Amazing," I said. "What about his angel? Can you tell me about him? Was Abraham's angel with him his whole life?"

**Yes. No listener would move when the angel talked because his name was holy. It was Nathan. My large jaw dropped.**

Josiah jumped off the couch and charged down the hall. Meanwhile, I googled *Nathan* and discovered it's a Hebrew name that means "gift from God." Of course it did.

I gave Josiah some room time and then eagerly peeked in. "Want to talk more about it?"

He vibrated his lower lip and followed me to the couch. There, he continued right where he'd left off, as if he'd never stopped.

**I knew it was my great night to hear Nathan say he bolstered Abraham Lincoln. Right then he said, "Boy of God's fire, you have big angel Ronda to bolster you. Is your name Josiah?"**

**I said, "Yes."**

**He said, "You have big pages to fill, but you have big power to land on people too." He basically named me big huge boy in this day to just light God's fire in his people again.**

**He was about nine feet tall. He was muscular. He kind of looks like Jesus but he wasn't. He had a beard like Jesus though. He wore mighty, long, gold-plated armor. He never had wings, or if he did it was not evident to me. Armor said he was like a warring angel.**

My heart pounded at these delicious slices of heaven. What the angel said to Josiah reminded me of what the Lord said in Jeremiah 1. I looked up verses 4 through 9. "Hey Josiah, listen to these verses."

"The word of the LORD came to me, saying, 'Before I formed you in the womb I knew you, before you were born I set you apart; I appointed you as a prophet to the nations.' 'Alas, Sovereign LORD,' I said, 'I do not know how to speak; I am too young.' But the LORD said to me, 'Do not say, I am too young. You must go to everyone I send you to and say whatever I command you. Do not be afraid of them, for I am with you and will rescue you,' declares the LORD. Then the LORD reached out his hand and touched my mouth and said to me, 'I have put my words in your mouth.'"

"JoJo," I said, rubbing his back, "do you realize how incredible this is?"

**This very night, we have big jobs and big angels hold us up to make it so. I'm my own long-living self with Holy Spirit and my long-living mated angel moving my life in great service made in love. This is very nice to know.**

I gazed at his eyes through his crooked glasses and let his gentle smile warm me to the core. *Purpose,* I thought, *truly means everything.*

I love it, Mom, when Jesus kisses my face. We hold hands, and we value halls of hope together. Halls of hope are beauty yet to happen. King Jesus walks with me down the hope hall, seeing my future.

Run to the dazzling river of life. You come out like a dry man, only saturated in plans.

His big gate is pearl. Because he is the Lord of past loud seas, mighty mountains, and long miles of land, he gets a big pearl from his own hand!

Natural streets are gold but clear, because they are so pure. No one gets past a pearly gate without Jesus housing their name. The Book of Life is in him, you see. God looks at him and sees you or me.

These words and experiences—oh my goodness. I felt like I'd just jumped into the river of God's love and been engulfed in the fresh wash of a wave.

One Sunday afternoon, I decided to ask Josiah a relevant question I'd been mulling around in my head. "So you've seen Auntie up there, right? I imagine you've seen other relatives too?"

I see them all the time. Family is so important I am always trying to find them so I can say hello.

I saw first my Grandpa Ken. It is my mom's dad. He must have been so proud because he named me his nice big grandson to lots of people. After my seeing Grandpa Ken, I saw my Grandma Mary Anderson and Grandpa Rusty.

I shook my head in disbelief. "That's my grandma and grandpa. You've never even met them on earth. Wow, you're just full of surprises. Who else did you see?"

I saw Uncle Dean, Grandpa Cullen, and Grandma Mary Cullen. I saw Grandpa Shea, and I saw Auntie.

There she was again. Auntie. The relative who had spring-boarded this whole thing into action. Our lives would never be the same since the day Josiah first wrote her name.

**I saw limitless ancestors on your side and Dad's that you have never even known in your life. Grandma Alma and Grandpa John, yes. It was all of our big family there.**

**Ken, my grandpa, liked to pass by, and he said, "My boy!" He was at my little going and coming place on my light path thing like a cable car. He invited my other family, all gathered.**

**It was joyful party in this big, life-sized park, Mom. Limitless family, Mom. Had a big hello and joyful ability to part with kisses.**

"Josiah, this is incredible. Do they talk to you?"

**Well, I'm here still on earth and they are not, so they like to face me and know how people are. Justly, they like me to tell people things too.**

**As long as they are on a wide balcony, they look down sometimes on our big laughter of births and weddings or nice bold moves toward God.**

I imagined my brother, father, and Auntie, all looking down at me, cheering me on as I grew in faith and moved closer to God.

*Oh Father, you aren't just a good gift giver. You're an awesome gap filler. Thank you for these last days where you reveal your mysteries. And thank you for using the foolish things to confound the wise. Just thank you.*

## 20

# Trinity Talk

> "Holy is this God, entirely worthy. Total in love.
> He's the farthest moving Father,
> but the most seated ruler."
> – Josiah Cullen

**God wants to show you about the triune God now, Mom.**
I straightened on the couch. If I wasn't fully awake before, I was now.

**In the Trinity, the Father is the manager. The Son is the lover of operations. Holy Spirit is worker. So it's the three-in-one getting things done.**

**The world was created only by three functions that went like this: Father thought it. Son loved it. Holy Spirit carried out the plan. That is how Trinity works, Mom. Father, Son, Holy Spirit lack nothing. And they all talk together about how things should go. Life is simple if you know he is Papa. He is Healer. He is Helper.**

"Josiah, that's wild. In just a few sentences, you've unraveled one of the greatest mysteries of the church."

**Man must voice, "Father, what do you think? Jesus, what do you love? Spirit, what should we do about it?" This is your mission: do what Father thinks and what Jesus loves and what Spirit tells.**

I thought about the first chapter of John. "In the beginning was the Word, and the Word was with God, and the Word was

God … The Word became flesh and made his dwelling among us"
(John 1:1, 14). I'd never seen all these little pieces so beautifully and
clearly connected. I felt like I was in a hot air balloon that had just
been fired up higher and higher.

"So what does God manage?" I asked.

**He manages it all, old and new. You get it, Mom?**

"And Jesus? What about him?"

**He is love. He saves. He joins all to the Father. He builds a
bridge. Mom, it is big to love like this.**

"Hmm, I see that. This is awesome, wild, and incredible. How
about the Holy Spirit?"

**Holy Spirit likes nothing more than to language our own jails
to open them. Holy Spirit works to get us to think like God and to
host his mighty desires in our own bodies.**

**Holy Spirit is verifying my own joy as I bring my jails to his
eyes. I'm so hit sometimes with facing days with no words. I feel
so planted in misery. I'm not mighty to ponder him as my lifeline
in times I'm sad.**

*Facing days with no words?* My heart sank. To resurrect my
spirit, I focused on the truth of Josiah's uplifting words. In spite
of human misery or "jails," the Holy Spirit lived and breathed to
verify my ever-existing joy. Knowing this, how could I not focus
on the bigger, better picture? Crumbling to my knees, I broke into
songs of heartfelt worship to the Father, Spirit, and Son, telling
God how much I loved and adored him. How much I would lay
my life before him.

God in his goodness had let Josiah see each member of the
Godhead. He had seen them distinctly separate yet flowing
together in unity. His words reminded me of what the Bible said
about God speaking the world into existence while the Holy Spirit,
an active participant, hovered over the surface of the deep. And
how Jesus, the Word who was God and with God, had already
loved us enough to die for us. He was slain before the foundations
of the earth (Revelation 13:8).

I'd always been taught to see the Trinity like liquid, vapor, and ice, three different forms of the same thing, so this brought my understanding to a whole new level, piquing my desire to know more.

Sometimes Josiah poured truth in drops; other times, it gushed out like water from a fire hose. One crisp fall afternoon as we walked along a favorite nearby lake, I found myself wondering how my spotty communication with my dad might have negatively affected my feelings about my heavenly Father.

Josiah's mind and body seemed extra calm, so when I saw an empty wooden bench, I seized the opportunity.

"JoJo, you do such a fabulous job explaining things. Can you describe Papa God a little more? Maybe even tell me what he looks like?"

**Mom, clarity is so nice. My world in his hands. Tune to his laugh and you will laugh. God is demonstrating "father" in every movement of his life. Gentle Father, joyful one, bold in every way, but gentle toward people who are faced with sin. He funded himself to help the world voice faith again.**

**The Father is everywhere. He faces you wherever you are, whoever you are! If he needs to stand, he is loudly saying, "Forces, move this instant! I am God, like it or not. My world is to be this way, not that, so you will be still, forces of Satan! Move this loud mountain now!" Then, slingshot! Boom! Now it is over. So voiced God like it was a mountain made to nothing.**

I loved focusing on God's power, but wanted to understand something else. "Josiah, how close do you get to God?"

**"Hurry to my lap," he says. "Richly you are a future mouth of my world, Josiah. Present my words that Father is tremendously watching over you, children." Most wrestle for years with this God. No, don't! Mostly just mouth, "I need you, Father."**

**Slowly he fills my soul with orders to be a friend to the friendless, to heal the sick, to voice deliverance to the slaves. He**

is powerful, so he is like forceful, but meek too. Real mushy, so he is like Dad, but so strong to be like deity.

Josiah kept pulling away his hand so he could strum his fingers on the rugged wooden slabs of the bench, while I kept gently redirecting him back.

Mom, he is ardently wonderful. Wrathful he is not toward people. He loves them all. He stirs them so they could choose him to be Father. He says, "Black little days that man listens to Satan make me tremendously sad." He is like a father wanting to help, but his welcome is to call for him.

His stones of fire are his lit-up middle. He glows loud, luscious colors to say, "Truth is truth. Order is order. Holy is holy." The stones are the standard everything rests on. It is his heart. Stones of truth.

Holy is this God, entirely worthy. Rich in his latter days. Rich in his former days. Loud in the gates. Loud in the mountains. Loud in pounding thunder. But soft inside. Fun. Matchless mapper to your design. Slow to anger, quick to love. He is like Dad, like Father, like Papa.

He loves to say, "You really dare me to out-love my Son? It is on! I dare him too to out-love me. It's a competition. The match has been tied for millennia."

People passed and dogs barked, but I didn't look up. I could barely move. *What would happen*, I wondered, *if Joe and I tapped into the Father's ways and spent our whole lives trying to selflessly out-love each other? Life would surely be more joyful and free.*

"Josiah, this is awesome." I felt almost weak with excitement, and I wondered how much longer he'd be willing to stay sitting. "Can you tell me about Jesus?"

Oh, he is timeless. He is mighty. He is justice. He is the pied piper of the delivered, daily working to call out mice that steal your peace.

Back in heaven, Jesus is like a boyish, original, spiritual, joyful guy who is laughing all the time. Men say that slim Jesus is tentative. No, he is masculine, strong, and a leader. Like his full-bodied stature is much like men who strongly work out. He is tremendously mean to demons to say, "Leave my people alone or you stir my tremendous roar!"

Jesus is stunning to look to, transcendent in his dunamis power. His eyes are blue like seas are inside of them. They are transitioning from sea to fire to luscious meadows to stunning under moss of trees to a luring turning of holding your image in the pupil, like you are the apple of his eye.

The sunlight suddenly danced in Josiah's eyes. I felt the warmth from his body. Hugged in this special moment as he continued.

Sometimes he wears a crown. Mostly when he listens to me, he trades a crown for a landing of just hair to be informal with me, I guess. To tell me secrets like my worn-in friend to him. To hear his thoughts, name his mandates, to voice missions to me where he says, "Wrestle with this, will you?" And then he says, "Tell me your ideas too. I like to hear them so much."

He wears spendy, king clothes when he is not in a white robe. The white robe has a sash that is triumphant to signify his spiritual mission to help us, to heal us, to lead us. It voices the musing on his mind, and the colors of the sash differ depending on which one he is discussing.

The green is healing, and the sound is thoughts of healing on his heart right now. So, remember, a three-strand cord—mind, heart, and words—is the margins of a miracle. The red sash triggers the leading of simple destiny to line up to the red blood of Jesus. The last one is purple.

He jumped, and his hand shot up and began to crane the air left and right like the periscope on a submarine.

"Josiah," I said, pulling him down. "This is absolutely blowing me away. Please keep going."

Jesus' hands tell a story of troubles over. His hands are pierced to be holy to God forever. Only wisdom knows this is the reason he still has the holes in his hands and feet.

Picture the Lamb. He says, "Teach my people that I had to be crucified like that. For I am now so pierced still to say, where is mysterious death? It is not yours to bear because I took it so you can be so heaven bound that your spirit can be free while on earth. You get to enjoy all of eternity with me. I am tremendous in my world. I am not just a joyful tale. Try living a mysterious, working, blaring, full life, and you will have both kinds of blessings given to you because you belong to my world. I am not shy to say my world belongs to you on earth as well. It is true. I am now hiring faithful people that are helpmates to me."

So voice the little hands to say, "Pick me, Jesus! I am that person who will partner with your plan to be the fullness of miracles in this earth."

Wings of glory fluttered inside, and I had no choice but to respond. *Pick me, Jesus! I'll partner with your plan.* Enwrapped with joy, I shut off the iPad and gave my arms a stretch. "Okay, let's go," I said.

We started toward the car, but then I steered us to the ice cream shop to give Josiah a surprise. A little fun fuel before he might unpack more mysteries.

As we sat outside at a picnic table, he spooned huge chunks of vanilla in his mouth. Oh well. At least I never had to tell him not to talk with his mouth full.

"Hey, Josiah," I said, tapping the iPad, "could you please tell me more about the Holy Spirit?"

You see, he is like fire, much like destiny welling up in your soul. Holy Spirit entirely stirs up love for Jesus and Father.

The picture people have of Holy Spirit is too reasonable. Lots of men think he is a fast, numb spirit using a fast miracle here and there to voice, "I'm here." No, he is not a numb spirit. He is the life daily given to us to live musically stirred by God in this earth. When Holy Spirit is in you, fast joys help you befriend a simple, daring, fun life.

**Listen to this. Life is spirit. Richly, why not have a spirit that is fully world class? The mighty God in your body!**

Josiah flowed with the passion of a preacher, and I could almost hear the volume rise and fall in his voice.

**Holy Spirit is like fast hope, dangerous joy, shaking passion, model of peace, listener of the daily world. It is true. He is the listening ear of prayers never spoken out. He prays, "Round it out, Father, what this person really means when they pray is this …" So he fast tells God the real you.**

**The Spirit is joking, fun, musing, classy, wordy, stirred, blaring motion inside of your churches. He is the full-time desire of your heart.**

**Since Spirit is life, he is in all of us—past, present, and future, but praise the nurtured choice: he is either joyfully received or loudly rejected in homes of the heart.**

**To be filled with Spirit is to be filled with glory. I love original Spirit loudly stirring my story, Mom. He is my song to this world.**

"Whew," I said, dabbing his face with a napkin. "I feel like shouting. It's either time to move on or time to get saved all over again."

I grabbed his hand as we crossed the parking lot. We stepped onto the walking path, and as the breeze tossed my hair, I inhaled the cool, leafy scent of fall.

We walked a ways. "Hey, look," I said. "There's a nice bench next to a monument. Let's sit down and drink our water bottles." As soon as we did, I asked if he had anything else he wanted to share.

**Holy Spirit is fire in and fire out. He is why we are the light of the world.**

**To say you are seated in heavenly places with God is to say the Spirit of God is seated in heaven, but he is also seated inside of you.**

**Under Spirit is truth. Order is truth. Simplicity is truth. Obedience is truth. Love is truth. Ride this life out in spirit and**

**in truth. And the paper Bible dancing on your hands to say, "I see this word alive and active and sharper than a double-edged sword."**

**You are the fullness of God in Christ. Work it out.**

I laughed. Work it out. Yeah, right. Like a simple math equation. I gave him a gentle hug, and it was time to call it a day. Did my eight-year-old son have any idea how these revelations boggled my mind? My son who I read to from the Children's Bible was now introducing me to the fullness of the Trinity. My son who I didn't think would ever be able to connect with me on earth kept connecting with God in heaven.

A carefree couple swung their little boy in the air by the hands while clouds crawled across the sky like they'd been moving forever. The world felt suddenly smaller—and God, all three parts of him, more embraceable.

Even with a front-row seat into God's nature, something told me that, like the bleeding woman who touched the edge of the Lord's garment, I had barely scraped the edge of the surface.

## 21

# High Places

"This bold hand is raised to
the strong tower of he who sees."
– Josiah Cullen

I felt like a Molly Maid as I scurried downstairs attacking dust bunnies with my feather-wand. I'd heard there might be a storm, so I stole glances at the television to catch the weather.

Suddenly, the anchorman cut short, and the television made an abrupt switch. I set down my duster and stepped closer to catch the special story. Of all things, it turned out to be a promotion for a silent retreat. Strangely, the channel switched abruptly back to the news. I stepped closer to the screen, trying to remember the name of the retreat place. Something with the word *pacem* in it. I remembered *pacem* from a choir song, because in Latin it meant "peace."

*Lord, are you trying to tell me something? Because if you are, I'm listening.*

I'd been asking him to sharpen my ears to his voice. It's one thing to hear the music, quite another to press in and distinguish the notes.

I had no idea what God meant by this *pacem* place, but I sure knew a tug from the Lord when I felt one.

The next day, I sipped a latte at Caribou and prayed for wisdom about the retreat as I googled *pacem*. Bingo. Pacem in Terris, or

"Peace on Earth." Their website described the place as a hermitage with multiple cabins spread out over sixty acres. Wouldn't you know, it was only an hour away. I hadn't been looking for a getaway, but I had been wanting to seek God about my future in ministry. Could this be a good place for me to tune out life's distractions and pray in solitude like Jesus did?

When I mentioned the idea to Joe, he laughed. "You—stay silent for that long?"

"Hey, watch it." I gave him a playful punch.

"It's up to you," he said. "The time alone would probably do you good."

I took that as a green light and signed up to go from a Tuesday to Friday during the first week in June.

When I shared my plans with a few trusted friends, I didn't expect e-mails. I certainly didn't expect anyone to have a dream about me.

*Dear Tahni. This doesn't happen to me often, but I had a dream about you and I'm not sure if you know what this means.*

*You stood high on a beautiful green, grassy hill looking down on other smaller green, grassy hills. The sky was clear with no clouds. I could see your heart had been turned to pure gold, beating full of passion.*

*As you spoke, your words spelled out in front of you, words in the air floating up and then turning to water drops like fountain water into the grassy hill below you.*

*Jen*

When a second e-mail came from my Facebook friend Michelle, I thought I'd better pay attention.

*Tahni, as I began to pray for you, I saw a flower opening. Its petals unfolded specifically "in order." Then the Lord said to me, "Things that bloom in order are of me. She is well with this."*

*I then saw a stream with grass growing on the bank in a valley. I could see a specific lone flower. It was white with four petals. The*

Lord said, *"Know not where this is planted? It is planted on fertile ground."*

*He then took me to a high mountain with sand on its peak. In the sand was drawn the flower that had been in the valley near the stream. "Ask Tahni this," he said. "How did one draw this here?"*

I read the letter to Josiah, and when I asked him what he thought, he didn't hesitate.

**The flower is picture of a mom each day as a praying best gem. Demons can't be in high places.**

Demons can't be in high places? Did he mean that you can't find demons in high places or that God doesn't want them to be in high places?

The morning I arrived at Pacem in Terris, dark clouds hung over a misting sky, but so did an umbrella of trees.

Stepping out of my car, I shivered. It felt more like October than June, but as I started up the long, winding brick path to the building, God's warm peace settled over me like an unbroken canopy of strength.

I opened the old heavy door and made my way down an empty hall where classy sculptures and paintings lined bright, welcoming walls. Seeing the open door to a chapel, I peeked inside. That's when I heard a voice behind me.

"Hello." An older lady with a wide smile introduced herself and led me to the orientation room. There, a man met me.

"Hi, I'm Justin. This is for you." He looked at me with kind eyes as he unveiled a basket with Wisconsin cheese, an orange, a bran muffin, a loaf of bread, and two ripe red apples. "Enjoy. There's a lot of flexibility here. In the evenings, you can come back to the building and join the others for dinner, or you can fast or do whatever you like. We don't have any cell phone service or Wi-Fi, but we do have a landline for emergencies."

I made one last call to Joe. Then I gave Justin my suitcase, he loaded it onto his Bronco, and off we went to my cabin.

"There's the outhouse," he said cheerfully. "And there it is—your hermitage. Each log cabin has a different name, and yours is St. John the Beloved."

He dropped my suitcase on the porch, creaked open the door, and nodded at the rocking chair in front of a large open window. "Sometimes you just have to rock it out, and this is the place to do it. Rock it out, pray it out, scream it out, and then get quiet before God. Here's a pen and notebook for journaling. Everything else should be in the cabin."

I thanked him and waved. Then I tried to figure out what to do next. The room came equipped with water bottles, a basin, kettle, single burner for tea and coffee, a propane light on the wall, a cross, a picture of Jesus, a kneeler, a Bible, a couple votives, a small screened porch, and of course, that lovely large window that looked out to the woods.

*Hi, God. I'm here. I made it. Hey, how's it going? You know, I really look forward to hearing from you.*

The silence screamed. Alone time with God. Yikes. I slipped into my jammies, made myself a cup of tea, and did what almost any mother with a slice of time alone would do—I crashed.

A couple hours later I awoke with a brand-new tune in my head, complete with lyrics. My first song. What a gift from God. I kept repeating it, so I wouldn't forget it.

Instead of joining the others for dinner, I feasted on the writings of John the Beloved. Was he watching me right now from heaven? Did he see his name on the door?

*Goodnight, Daddy. I'm going to blow out the light now. Please don't let me be spooked by noises, bugs, critters, and especially not by my own imagination. Thanks.*

The next day greeted me with the gentle sound of raindrops. Stepping onto the porch, I inhaled the fresh smell of wet foliage. The forest glimmered with life. Birds perched while rays of light broke through clouds, streaming through glistening leaves plump with water droplets.

I thought back to my first RPM training with Erika. "Tahni, talk to him like he's blind."

That's when I took Josiah to a park and talked about the veins on leaves. These days, he paid more attention to details than I did—both the seen and the unseen—and I could hardly keep up with him.

*God of all creation, I worship you ...*

I prayed for hours on my screened-in porch. Birds sang, leaves rustled, and I didn't have any visitors except the occasional squirrel.

I picked up a copy of the cabin Bible, a Catholic one, and leafed through. Wow. It had more books than I was used to. I searched the table of contents for Tobit, the book that mentioned the angel Raphael who brought healing. As I skimmed through, I noticed something about people offering sacrifices to idols in "high places." Yuck. I'd read about that kind of detestable practice in the Old Testament, and it always sounded so foreign and strange. Had God pointed this out so I would ponder Josiah's words?

I grabbed my own Bible, and using my concordance, I identified all the verses that mentioned high places. By flickering lamplight, I pored over Scriptures like the people of old.

I jumped from king to king, noting how most of them had allowed demonic idols to exist in high places even though God had clearly wanted them torn down. When I came to 2 Kings, I saw something wild. Josiah, who became king at eight years old, was the first king to remove all the shrines in the high places! He was also considered one of the most righteous kings because he restored the ways of the Lord.

I knelt on the floor. *Oh God, no one could take your rightful high place. No demon in hell. No power on earth. I exalt you, King Jesus. There is none beside you.*

A Bible verse popped into my mind. "Above all else, guard your heart, for everything you do flows from it" (Proverbs 4:23).

God had talked to me in the past about watching the gates of my heart. For some reason, I felt like he wanted me to do some house-cleaning again. The Holy Spirit prompted me to tear down any of my own high places, any thoughts that might have exalted themselves against the knowledge of Jesus.

Josiah had written a fascinating word about the importance of the heart. I scrolled back to it on the iPad, wondering how long I'd have it before it ran out of charge.

**Make a vine to your head from your heart and build a trellis with your spine. See the art of baptism? It is heart under the water first, then your mind laughing toward this renewal.**

**King Jesus said vines are your heart's salutations toward sending foliage, bringing all the answers you need from your heart. Grapevines are heart vines. Prune your heart. It is entirely the circulatory system. Grapevines are the capillaries. Grapes are the cells.**

**Jesus gardens your heart to be pruned. Man is the sender of such leaves up to his brain. Make the heart right first. Make the brain produce fruit. Name your pruned heart to be a new messenger to your brain. Send up major vines. Actions voice your pruned heart.**

An old Scripture song flowed freely and naturally from my lips. "Create in me a clean heart, O God; and renew a right spirit within me."

My prayer time felt like tossing rocks of thoughts on water. Concentric circles growing outward, wider and wider. I prayed for me, then for my family, my church, my city, and my society.

I groaned, rocked, paced, knelt, laughed, cried, and dropped flat out on my face. I declared, decreed, warred, and of course, waited. God had called me to partner with him, and heaven forbid I miss even a sliver of his thoughts. No. I wanted his very heartbeat.

Over the last three decades, God had taught me a lot about prayer. But lately, he'd used my pint-sized little messenger to blow the lid off my understanding. Finally resting my head on the bed pillow, I pondered Josiah's recent words.

Jog to the phone and call your mom. This is the space between you and your mom bridged. So it is with bridging heaven to earth. The call is pictured as being so far, but it is so close. The Lord of life is closer than your breath.

People order stuff off the Internet, right? It is a blunt list of things to line your shelf to your home, and it comes to you, right? So it is with God. Order from his list and you will get his list. Order from the market of your nemesis and you will get their list.

But say you get a wrong package delivered to you. You order up a package from God, and they get there first with their package. You didn't order that, so reject it by not allowing it originally.

Maybe the one delivering your package works you over so much to take it. If you are thinking how it could fit into your world, you accept it because you didn't know what to do with it otherwise. Learn to hand it back with a "no way." Get your slip to return to sender—wrong address on those packages!

Limit the tentative prayers.

If you order something from God's list, you should get it. If you don't right away, you should make another call and ask why. Order it up again. Then it will be spoken to the warehouse that you want that thing, and checked it is on God's list for you to have it. Miscellaneous sleet, rain, or snow delivery conditions will not keep heaven from delivering a package that is resting with assurance that it left God's outbox.

One more thing. You may be waiting on a package. You get one, and open it eagerly in your home. But you see it is not what you ordered, so you send it back, right? Well, you could just handle it on the outside, look at the ID, shake the package first to see what is inside. If it sounds like wholeness, receive it. If it sounds broken, don't receive it. Send it back immediately to the very passionate channel that keeps sending you stuff you didn't order, sparing no expense to hit you over and over. Send them back to the original sender, and don't let them stay for a moment.

I had always been fascinated with Daniel 10. Daniel had been so overwhelmed by an angelic visitation that he fell asleep and experienced the rest of his revelation in a vision. As God pulled back the heavenly veil, the angel in the vision told Daniel that his request for understanding had been heard from the first day Daniel humbly prayed.

Not only that, but when the angel tried to bring Daniel heavenly help, a demon, the prince of Persia, battled against Daniel's angel for twenty-one days. God saw this happen and sent the angel Michael, one of the chief princes, to assist Daniel's warring angel and get the message to Daniel.

What a great chapter to shed light on the hidden workings of the spiritual world.

On my last day, the sun made its biggest and best appearance, transforming the place with its warmth and radiance. What a perfect day to take a prayer-walk along green-canopied paths dotted with little groupings of purple flowers.

I found a pond with reeds, cattails, and lily pads, and skipped a stone. Then, kneeling by a large wooden cross, I drank in a deep breath and exhaled my praise.

*At your name, Lord Jesus, every knee will one day bow and every tongue will confess that you are Lord to the glory of God the Father.*

When I stood and walked farther, I saw a bench and wondered what Josiah would say if he were here. Surprises and mysteries kept spilling out of him with ever-increasing acceleration, clarity, and maturity. Frankly, I felt so small when it came to knowing what God wanted me to do with all this. But like my mom said, God would show me.

When I returned home, I wondered again about the high places and felt a sudden pull to check something out.

I opened Google and typed, *What is the highest point in Minneapolis?* Of all things, "Witch's Hat Water Tower" appeared, with a picture of its pointy-hat architecture. Reading on, I discovered it was no longer a water tower, but rather a historic site celebrating its one-hundredth anniversary. A separate online pagan newsletter described witches and pagans gathering under the shadow of this particular tower to make decrees over the city and waterways.

My heart skipped. Wait a minute. God had shown me the importance of owning the gates, because whoever owns the gates owns the city. Why should the people from the kingdom of darkness be making decrees over our land? Did Christians even know about this? What could I personally do about it?

Several months later, just a few days before Halloween, my mom visited from Washington. She sat with Josiah, watching him punch out words.

**Are you going to busy the tubular tent in Minneapolis? Steal the party hat off the tower. Much lunging in prayer demands the Jenga to fall and tricks to be treated to luminous Jesus. "Rise up," Jesus tells me, "and sturdy your legs, for I'm taking dinner to my people in Minneapolis. With your mustard seed of faith, it will be roses tomorrow to stun demons from their looking over."**

I looked at my mom. "Oh my gosh. I'd forgotten about the tower. I never even said anything to him about it. He does this all the time … He just knows things."

"Josiah, are you trying to say we're supposed to go there?"

**Yes, go there.**

My throat felt dry. I'd heard stories about people who dared to mess with the devil, and let's just say I didn't want the things that happened to them to happen to me.

But what if God wanted me to go there? What if he planned to use the silent retreat to prepare me? Could this have anything to do with my friends' dreams and visions of me standing in the high places looking down? And what about that lady who saw me raising a silver trumpet to break open the atmosphere? Even more, what about my own realistic dream?

Recently, I'd had a dream where my mom and I went to a mental institution to pray for people—and what a sight. Everybody looked too tired and drugged up to even have a conversation.

A nurse whispered, "You might think everything looks calm and fine ... but just wait until the demon shows up."

Mom and I knew we had a choice. We could stay and pray, or we could make a fast getaway. We chose to pray.

Then, as we gathered around a young man, it happened. A large demonic creature emerged from behind the couch. It had long fingernails and brown patchy hair like a wolfman. Saliva dripped from its mouth as it lunged toward me, snarling and growling.

"Stop your show!" I ordered. "In the name of Jesus Christ, I command you to let these people go!"

Instantly, the huge creature shrunk into a tiny thing that looked like a cross between a flamingo and a dodo bird.

When I woke up, I knew God had given me an entirely different picture of Satan and demons. I saw them as spirit beings who worked through fear, deception, and intimidation. Josiah called it "sham authority." My dream showed me that when the Enemy clawed for authority, I had nothing to fear because I had God's true authority.

So now what did God want us to do? What if Minneapolis had opened the wrong package? Did God want to send something better?

Mom and I prayed and fasted until sundown. Then God said, "Go." Mom phoned a few trusted prayer partners to pray for us. I called Sue Rampi, and Sue called her intercessor and missionary friend, Jeanette.

The following morning, the four of us stood at the start of a steep path leading up to the base of the Witch's Hat Tower. I had no idea what was going to happen, but I felt united with these mothers of the faith, and marveled at how God had set this all up.

Sue and Jeanette had huge hearts for their city. They'd been missionaries in the past, so they'd witnessed how spiritual oppression and deception could overwhelm people in specific territories and regions.

I gave everybody a tight hug. "Thanks for being crazy enough to step out into the unknown."

Mom had knee issues, so she opted to stay on a bench at the bottom with Sue. From the moment I'd introduced the two of them, they'd hit it off like long lost friends.

Jeanette and I hiked up the long steep path to the base of the tower. As worship music rose from my iPad, we walked around and around the tower like it was the walls of Jericho. We felt energized by Mom and Sue's fervent prayers below. On this brisk overcast morning, we could see the whole city. As I prayed aloud, I imagined Jesus standing over Jerusalem, aching for change.

"God, we're here to obey and stand in the gap for the broken, the hungry, and the helpless. We pray for the seven mountains of society—for business, government, media, arts and entertainment, education, the family, and religion. We're sorry for all the areas where we've rejected you and traded truth for a lie.

"We pray for all leaders in authority. May they echo your heart in their decisions. Change hearts of greed, lust, and selfish ambition into hearts of generosity, purity, and compassion. We release light to displace the kingdom of darkness.

"Banish the evil spirits behind terrorism, crime, abortion, and sex trafficking. We know your heart breaks for the people bound and victimized by these deceiving, destructive spirits. Our battle is not against flesh and blood, but against the rulers, against the authorities, against the powers of this dark world and against the spiritual forces of evil in the heavenly realms. We tear down idols in the high places, dismantling all demonic principalities over the city gates, and we cancel all witchcraft, curses, and decrees. We partner with angels to repossess the gates for good, not evil. Lift up your heads, you gates. Lift them up, you ancient doors, that the King of glory may come in."

Two large birds flew through the arched openings in the tower, swiftly from one side to the other. Then I noticed a peculiar dot of light reflecting off a distant building. We hardly paid attention to people walking and jogging by, but they probably paid attention to us.

"Hello," I said to a smiling couple before refocusing on our purpose.

"God, you reign. It says in Isaiah 52:7, 'How beautiful on the mountains are the feet of those who bring good news, who proclaim peace, who bring good tidings, who proclaim salvation, who say to Zion, "Your God reigns!"' Reigning Father, reign in Minneapolis. May your kingdom come, your will be done, on earth as it is in heaven.

"We unleash your love, Lord. We break bondages, disband all lying spirits, and command all blinders to fall off, in Jesus' name. Loving Father, thank you that you've come to set the captives free. Jesus, you are the way, the truth, and the life. Nobody comes to the Father except through you. Bring healing to all those who are homeless, exploited, and lonely. Strengthen the pastors, believers, and laborers as they do your work.

"Jesus, touch broken bodies of people who are at the end of their rope. Thank you, that by your stripes we are healed. Bring healing to those with all kinds of disabilities and disorders. Stop this ever-growing epidemic of autism. Knock it clear off the map. We bind and break off all curses, and we speak healing and blessing over this land.

"Hosts of heaven, reach the hearts of those who are far from you. May your message spread rapidly and be widely honored in this city. Bring revival!"

That night, as I tucked Josiah in bed, I realized that my prayers had actually helped my heart grow bigger for the city.

"Go ahead, JoJo," I said. "Any quick final thoughts?"

**It was a tremendous ruin that used music to yell truths to fend for freedom. Be absolutely joyful in all things. Joy turns the tables on enemies of Jesus. Turn up joy. Demons can't stand it. Rise up. Run to me. Trust me. Nurture joy.**

"Amen, and I love you," I said, giving him a squeeze.

I prayed as I headed to the living room to join Mom and Joe.

*I feel your stretch, Father. I don't know where we're going with this, but here I am, Lord. Send me.*

## 22

# Angels

"Get the Savior's artful, genuine view. We are daring warriors, but the Savior dealt a death blow two thousand years ago, spinning Satan's kingdom out of orbit."

– Josiah Cullen

*December 2013*

One day at McDonald's, Josiah became unusually quiet and stared at the wall.

"JoJo, a second ago you looked like you were starving, and now you aren't even eating your burger. You're just staring. What's up?"

**I do not want it. I stare at a stunning angel.**

"What? An angel? Where do you see an angel?"

**Over by the boat picture.**

A chill ran up my spine. "Okay. Why is it here?"

**It's on a best mission to visit us and is listening in on our conversation.**

"Listening in?" I said, looking toward the painting. "Uh … hi, angel."

**He says hi. Stunning angel is right here, and I want to touch it. I am awestruck. His original beauty is stunning.**

"Wow, 'stunning' says a lot, especially after everything you've been sharing about heaven. What does he look like?"

**His hair is running to his shoulders. The Torah is written on his sash.**

Could this get any wilder? Typical kids had imaginary friends, but I'd never heard of an imaginary friend with God's written instructions on his sash. "Honey, did he say or do anything?"

**The band is playing. It is life. It is truth. Ponder the truth. Lies are dangerous. Lies are broken at the spiritual level. Nurture trustworthy possibilities. Trouts are tuned to swim upstream, not downstream.**

**It is cold now, but living underwater is teeming with life, even though you can't see it. I present truths beneath the surface. Ice doesn't mean death. More life is on the way, like in trout season. Go upstream to the origin of coulds. Turn to the upstream songs where the Rock of Ages piles up stones of truth. Come upstream to reproduce.**

His words left me swimming, floating, soaring. We'd been watched. Talk about giving new meaning to the phrase, entertaining an angel unaware.

It happened again, the next time at the Children's Museum in the snack area.

"Look," Joe said. "Strange. Josiah is staring out the window, practically mesmerized. All I can see is a black man stepping out of his car and locking it. Hey, bud, what are you looking at?" Joe and I both watched close as the words came out.

**That guy is a Christian, and he just had his angel stand by his car. A stunning angel is at his car.**

Joe and I exchanged looks as I struggled to understand. Had the guy just prayed over his car or something? Had someone else prayed for his protection? Or did this particular angel just happen to regularly accompany him?

I thought of Psalm 34:7: "The angel of the *Lord* encamps around those who fear him, and he delivers them."

How wild to be so aware of Scripture coming to life. With Josiah around, I would never again be able to look at the natural world in the same light.

Over the next few days, I decided to talk more about angels. "How often do you see them?" I asked, retrieving a napkin from his mouth.

**I see angels very often. Maybe once a day in my waking hours. Like all the time in night hours. I see them in my house, in my jolly major living room, in mobilizing to places I might see angels eavesdropping on us. To look on angels is nice because they are hugging my life to plant me in my best places.**

**I hear angels more than I see them. To hear them is huge to me. Huge angels build me up to language my nice helping facts to let my mom know about things.**

"I love knowing these things," I said. "How big are they?"

**Small, medium, large, and gigantic.**

"Do we all get an angel from the time we're born? I mean, one that basically stays with us our whole life and helps us?"

**Way out there, yes! It is not just a myth. It is real. It is big to long for this understanding because guardian angels very much like you. They are so perfect for you. They get you. It is very nice to have a guardian angel.**

"The other day you mentioned some specific names of angels. Like Banfa, for example. What's he like?"

**Banfa is big angel of singing kind. He is making lots of artful applications of life solutions to join angels in looking for God's attitude on this earth. He was big to a larger cause. He was very much a ruling angel of solution for things with no known solution. He is a luminous light leader of the age of healing. It was big to just know he bangs a drum for autism in this world to be solved.**

You'd think I'd be used to this by now, but his words still shook me. "Okay, so you've also referred to Ronda as your guardian angel. Who is she? I didn't think there was such a thing as female angels."

**Male and female in heaven is not like on earth. It is not like a male and female parts thing. Angels insist on one thing, to look like us in some ways. It is like God. It is his image. His image is also this huge group of angels.**

Others might be looking like pointing ears and big mouths of animals kind of. Lion people kind of. It is hard to point out because they are so just different. Lots of big variety. Lots of colors. I'm just not mighty to look out of particulars because it is not my portion to handle it.

Ronda is my guardian angel. It is looking more female. It is very nice to me. It has very large wings. It is my angel to work in me, noting my life is bigger if my joy is bigger. Big Ronda is a great nine feet or so. It is fast to my side. It is great to justly make nasty demons move away from me as I pray. It is fighting for me all the time.

"Wow," I said. "It sounds like the strongest bodyguards on earth have nothing on these glory beings. It makes me wonder something else. A lot of Christians talk about spiritual warfare. Do you know how that works?"

Warfare is not mighty in my vocabulary. It is big demons being major because man is not being major in his life's job to plant and harvest in God's nimble ways. Lucifer is jogging around and building his palaces in purposeful points in his kingdom, but he is not our equal or our lord. He is a big brat and big liar.

Warfare is faithful humanity holding up Jesus against one guilty mandate of Lucifer who is hurrying to arrest our hands and feet. Our hands and feet are purposefully to name life to our world. He is very much in a fight with us, but this very idea is not like head-to-head combat. It is not him and his army against us and God's army. It is great big Savior insisting he is winner, and we are more than conquerors. It is not winning but guarding. I'm not fighting. I'm holding his ground.

"I need to remember that next time I face a battle," I said. "This is really good stuff. You've also written about an angel named Gamma, especially back when you first started writing."

Yes. This is Gamma. It is ten times gain. You get net gains with natural payback for issues nagging you in holy justice. Gamma duplicates blessing for your troubles.

Gamma is very huge, like maybe fifteen feet high. It looks

**like a female, but it has nothing factually to make it female. It just appears pretty. It is a great big reaping kind of angel. It reaps what is sown for you and gives you lots of joy. Gamma was not only in heaven but here too.**

"Wow," I said. "I won't pretend to understand all this, but it's very fascinating, and I'm totally listening. I was also wondering if you could tell me about Jehud?"

**Jehud was a great angel of praise. He awed me as he gated our family in praise to love Jesus more as our Lord. He was fire-like in his appearance. He acts to make our lighting to be natural as our great God saves our real lives while we praise. He was about six feet.**

**It is great to see your angels too, Mom, and Dad's, but it is only given to me just once in a while. It is very nice to see your angel politely making you love more, and Dad's angel making him think more like man of lighting of big joy.**

"Oh, Josiah," I said, squeezing his shoulder. "I don't know what to say sometimes. Thanks for sharing."

I decided to punch the angel names into Google and see what came up. I started with Banfa, the angel who supposedly took him to a place where they spoke Mandarin Chinese.

Wouldn't you know it, Banfa turned out to be a Chinese word for "a method or a way." It meant "solution," exactly what Josiah said that Banfa provides. These discoveries further fueled my curiosity.

The name Ronda meant "good spear." Perfect for a guardian angel.

And why wasn't I surprised that Jehud was more than a city in Israel? It meant "praising"—the very thing I wanted to do as I pondered these wild discoveries. Dropping to the couch, I lifted my hands, feeling small and big at the same time.

*I praise you, Father, Lord of heaven and earth, because you have hidden these things from the wise and learned, and revealed them to little children. Thank you for opening my eyes, and please continue to open them even more.*

## 23

# Sponsors and Factories

"I busted my heart open on a happy day,
ordering pie in the sky."

– Josiah Cullen

*March 2014*

After a fun museum tour of the flour tower at Gold Medal Flour's factory ruins, I needed a break. Joe stepped in line to buy me an espresso while Josiah, who had been writing about earthly factories, suddenly switched his focus to heavenly ones.

"Factories in heaven?" I said. "What do you mean?"

He brought his shoe to his face, and then flung it to the floor before he continued.

**The apple dare factory is the factory of God's rich opportunity to do something you wouldn't normally do. You get an apple from the machinery to take to the earth in angel helpers' hands to a person that needs to take a dare.**

"I'm confused," I said. "So this all starts with some kind of factory in heaven?"

**Factories are funny to explain. It looks like a factory inside, but it takes much less time to produce something. It is like you think it, and it is radically made before your eyes.**

"Whoa. Sounds bizarre. Are you sure?"

**You have to understand. The spirit is like the natural world,**

but it is more real than our world. Even so, dares are in apples, for instance, because they are sweet rewards to those who pick them, who try them.

I shook my head. "Dares are in apples?"

It is in an apple spiritually speaking. The person begins to feel a strong desire to take a daring leap to destiny's trials that make them need God more to accomplish such a feat. That is how it works.

Josiah's hand swung over his head like a talking puppet, then dropped back down.

Lots of people work at the apple dare factory to think of dares to voice musing to people for their next step. Orders come from stirred muses that say, "That person needs this. This person needs that. Make a good dare. Move them toward it."

The order is placed and put in a box, and angel messengers deliver the dares. Happily, they know if you will take the dare based on your choice while they are there in front of you. If you take it, they leave a sweet reward. If you don't, they bring it back.

We returned home for dinner, and Josiah and I resumed our couch talk while Joe watched from the side.

"I don't quite get it yet," I said. "You mentioned that orders are placed in heaven. How does that work?"

Sponsors line up at the feet of Father to say, "Please, Father, help my stirred-up world. It is daily worry that makes loved ones tremendously sad. Like faith is low, so Father, simply send your faith to them." An order is placed, and he sends faith to the earth by angels.

"It's mind-boggling to think of people in heaven actually working with angels," I said. "I doubt I could make a theological case for this, but in a strange kind of way, it makes sense. So if they're both part of heaven together, does that mean they're jointly aware of us on earth?"

He typed three words. **They see you.** Then he banged a few notes on his toy lion piano.

"Hey, this is good for us both. Please keep going." I knew he probably wanted to, but he needed a little help, so I led him back to the couch.

**They remember the storms when something bad happened, so they sponsor you to say, "Help them, Father."**

"Is that what Auntie did?"

**Auntie saw me struggling so much to see. She struggled to see. She had a brain but couldn't see to learn, so she was so sad as a kid. She was sad I was getting sad. She asked an angel to give me faith to present myself. So I was led to say, "I am not blind anymore to life."**

"So Auntie told an angel," I said, mesmerized. I knew Auntie had suffered from bouts of blindness all her life and that it kept her from being a teacher. How amazing to think that she was now helping others like us to see into these things.

**This is the daily work of sponsorship: to be more than what you thought you could be.**

**Rich, isn't it, Mom? Work in heaven is done for two reasons: one, it is for mansion work to prepare places for those who will present themselves one day in heaven; two, it is for helping those on earth. And sampling all of that is the delight of heaven dwellers.**

**So see that most stirred-up workers make the music to voice full-time faith to people in the earth again. Oh, I am so happy to tell you this. Our loved ones keep helping us down here. Ken is a slamming-fast apple dare operator. He makes apple dares.**

"My dad?" I said slowly. I tried to picture him watching us with a big smile while Josiah basically handed me enough apple dares for a whole basket. I tried to breathe. "Josiah, this blows my mind. What are some other people doing in heaven?"

**Dean works at a rich, original space that pours out world ideas that sound like innovative spare parts. He is the supervisor of innovative ideas to help ideas come to life, because in the**

earth, he helped people innovate their way of doing things so they could be successful.

"My brother?" Rattled, I barely had time to think before he started typing about my mom's mom.

**Mary Anderson sews broken hearts back together. That is what she does. Angel delivers it. The order is fulfilled when a sewn heart is received using faith to be made whole again in your soul. She knows whose heart it is that she is mending, and she lines it with words of life to say, "Think on these things: lovely, pure, good report, child. Sound it out and you will live again. So walk it out."**

**Mary had to do that on earth when she lost her son, Gordon, so she is stirring up others to walk it out. Like she turned to God, they will turn to God for sorrow to be mended. She mends hearts.**

I ran a hand through my hair and thought back to when Mom told me about her older brother Gordon's fatal car crash where he left behind three small children and a wife. You mean, just like in 2 Corinthians, Grandma Mary now comforts others with the comfort she received? Could that verse about comfort carry over to the heavenly dimensions? My mind couldn't spin any faster, and nothing could take my attention away from the iPad.

**Auntie liked good, healthy food, so she is a maker of good foods to this earth. She makes wheat, oat, raspberries, and lots of good tree molasses. She liked molasses.**

Well, he had that right too. Auntie had always been into health food, and she used to eat prime molasses on homemade cornbread.

**You remember she liked it. In heaven she makes good food to the earth to heal the land, heal the stomach, heal the proud system's produce to be more healing to people's bodies. Better food is what she spiritually releases.**

**Rusty is to befriend people, so he faithfully makes rich, original ranch prints.**

"Hey, wait!" I said. "Get back here!" Too late. He'd already twisted himself off of the couch, climbed the old wooden trunk in front of our window, and taken a high flying leap into the air. "Can you finish your sentence?" I grabbed his arm and gave him a tickle.

Finally, he collapsed on the couch, gave his hair a good tug, and went right back to writing.

**You see, I told you about ranch life. Rusty told me about it. Ranch life is the print he designed to send out to the earth.**

I stared, dumbfounded. "That word about horses came from my grandpa? No way."

But Josiah had already busied himself back to his toy piano. Meanwhile, I read the saved words he'd written weeks before.

**There are two ranches. One has four ponies and one has one horse. The ranch with four ponies are gain, pride, tarry, and self-majesty, pictured in the world today, trying to put people on the backs of those ponies. To rest on the back of the one horse— God's power—is to price his trails as the ones worth going on, to be broken in by obedience, not acting like you're something on your own.**

**A lot of people will say the pony ranch is their world. Well, not necessarily. You could live on the horse ranch on the back of the one horse that holds it all up. You say how tough the pony ranch is, but you wandered to that ranch. And it is hard there, so how about stay at the horse ranch instead of being dragged around by ponies?**

**On the horse ranch, it is richly working together to say, "I like it here, so I will stay here." You have all things on God's ranch to bring justice on this planet.**

Josiah's analogy spoke to me even more than when I first read it. Grandpa had raised Mom and her siblings on a horse ranch in South Dakota, so, in a strange way, it made sense that Grandpa would have a richer, deeper, fuller ranch job in heaven than the one he had on earth. Why wouldn't he design such a "print" for angels to release to earth?

One day after church, Josiah wanted to do something he enjoyed from time to time: paint a picture. He loaded his paintbrush with a big glob of red acrylic paint and made a long bright streak across the top of his paper.

"Nice sky," I said. It reminded me of the thin veil separating heaven from earth and how God had slowly been unzipping it.

"Ready to clean up?" I asked when he'd finished. "Here, let me wash the red off your hands."

I cleared off a spot for the iPad. "Josiah, I'm wondering how much our past relatives know about us?"

**Nothing is vague to our loved ones in heaven. It is known our basic fears and our high moments. It is not just out of sight, out of mind. Our loved ones find out about us.**

I cleared my throat. "So right now they could be watching us and working on our behalf? My dad along with everybody else?"

**A lot of people get to put their talents and gifts to work in heaven in the most perfect way for them to help on the earth. Ideas might be offered, justice might be offered, comfort might be offered, joy might be offered, and much more.**

**Obedient Mary Anderson makes rounds for her family all the time. She is daily before God with requests. She stirs faith for simple family to say:**

**"Line their life with faith, Father, so they can be pictures to your king. Each time daily worry is loud for them, they spike a fever in the Spirit, Lord. I am now asking you to send faith to Richard, Rosannah, Boyd, John, Sharon, and for Gordon's family, and all my children's families, to help them become children today before you like I am before you. Stir their hearts. Pick their lives to be daring, full to the brim with order, simplicity, and trust in you. Delight to bless them. Father, they richly will be my trout in the earth to swim upstream, not go downstream."**

"Amen," I said as a thought popped in my mind. Was it possible that the phrase "on earth as it is in heaven" meant more than

I'd previously considered? I asked Josiah, and he didn't hesitate to answer.

**It is a cloud of witnesses to say, "Run the race." It is the full-time daily work of the loud servants of God to dare their world in heaven to help their world on earth. This is the cycle of the saints of God. When you are in heaven, you are home. Does that make sense? I am now so rich in my world here and there, both at the same time.**

With that, Josiah slid under the table and made noises. "La, la, lee ..."

"Okay, let's move to the couch. Then maybe you can tell me how sponsors can see us." I helped him to his feet, and we fumbled over. Plopping down, he rocked back and forth before I guided his hand to the iPad.

**Loved ones see us by going to ledges on the unusual homes of heaven that have a porch of massive size. On these porches, many worlds part and they can see through the blackness to the earth. It is a blast of "what is happening back in my world at this time?" Angels go up and down a lot.**

"You mean like Jacob's dream of the angels going up and down the ladder?"

But I'd already lost him into play mode. He rolled like a wheel, leaving my thoughts spinning just as fast.

I knew from Scripture that God always keeps his eyes on us, so in one sense, wouldn't it be silly for people in heaven, who are fully with God, to stay clueless about what's happening on earth?

I grabbed my Bible for more answers, and when I came to 1 Samuel 28, I sat straighter. I'd almost forgotten that story.

King Saul was unable to hear from God in the usual ways, so he did something he shouldn't have done. He asked a medium to conjure the prophet Samuel, who had already died. In that brief exchange between Samuel and King Saul, Samuel knew full well what had happened on earth since his passing.

Could it be that in these last days, God wanted to pull back the veil on his own initiative and show us more? In the midst of my daily pain, these kinds of truths certainly made me more excited about my heavenly home.

Before school the next day, Josiah jumped right back into his discussion about sponsorship.

**Just like lighthouses bring ships into harbor, our loved ones hold our lives as being out in the sea. Love lets them see where the ship is on its bright course.**

**If it is not going into its designated path, it is being tossed in the waters. They might not know details, but they know if your faith is not holding you toward your lighthouse. They say, "This is my family member or my friend. It is very much my desire to see them in heaven."**

**I thought it was very natural to know these things, Mom. It is not? It is daring to just know Bible tells of this big idea. Answer is big if you see it.**

**Life in my limited earth is not all of life. It is eternity our hearts are made for. Our ninety mouthing years or less might seem long, but it is not our entire life. Our lives go on.**

His bus came to a stop in front of our house, so I gave him a quick hug and kiss and walked him outside. He had opened a wild, weird, and wonderful box, and I could hardly wait for the rest.

## 24

# Mansions

"Mansions are big and different and have friends
like striped cats and furry dogs that you knew as a kid.
I have a mansion already!"

– Josiah Cullen

*April 2014*

After school one day, Josiah and I made small talk about his teachers and subjects, until the topic suddenly switched to his favorite subject: heaven.

**Great big mansions are not motels or teepees or lodging like anything we have here. Mansions are boldly your life in multiple layers built into your outer home. This very idea that we have individual homes in heaven is really neat. Why? Because each person is different. Mansions are the personal expression of this person in house form.**

"Wow, that's wild. I can't wait. Any pets up there?"

**Felines you loved are felines you have. Joys of your long years as a kid, you get a bold, great, nice hug from. Just think of all you really liked. You will have it in your mansion.**

"Oh, okay. I prefer canines over felines, so I guess that means I'll see Fluffy, Tria, and Rags."

He rubbed his eyes. **Anonymously, your family asks for your great loves to be waiting for you. It is big to have a nice band** safely making your mansion so lovely even before you will ever see it.

At one fast family gathering, my grandpa Ken was bragging about my grandma's dolls. He said she was big to make these little dolls bit by bit out of her basement sewing room. It was basically her joy to make little dolls and little clothes.

"You know about the dolls?" I said, straightening. "How? What did you find out?"

He said you loved Hercermer so much, he was mightier than any of your dolls. He built you a nice bunk bed for your dolls. He built one big crib for Hercermer out of the bunk beds. You had a baby boy with blond hair in your doll room. He noticed it was like me, Mom. It was your favorite. Nothing but joy with Hercermer.

The iPad shook in my hand. How did he know about Hercermer?

It was building our family might even before I was born to have a doll like me, Mom. Real kid would come, but you loved this blond-headed doll. Was your Hercermer boy like me, Mom? Was Hercermer your best doll? All my baby gabbing was great naturally, wasn't it, Mom?

Baby gabbing. Oh my goodness, yes. His lively gusts of toddler words had melted my heart from day one. They had come to him with joy and much practice. *Mama, Daddy, cheese, no-no, JoJo, cookie, bumblebee.* Then they'd been ripped away by a thief, leaving a big, gaping hole.

I remembered Mom telling me about when she and Dad lost their business and couldn't afford Christmas gifts. I was only seven. Mom refused to take the grief lying down. She marched right to her sewing room and poured out her disappointment to God. That's when he reminded her of her motto: *You've got to take what you have and do something with it.*

Darting around the room, she found an old pattern and scraps of material, and she made her first dolls, Matthew and Mandy. The twenty-four-inch soft-sculpture dolls could have passed for twins.

Mom's misfortune turned over a profit at craft fairs, and the dolls also became great gifts for friends.

Two years later, Mom made me a blue-jean-clad baby with a Cabbage-Patch face who smiled beneath a mess of yellow yarn hair. My all-time favorite doll, Hercermer. My eyes returned to the iPad.

**Ken knew you liked him, so he made him for you like he remembered. Hercermer will be there.**

With that he darted to his room.

"Hey, wait! We aren't finished!" His words echoed through my mind as I chased after him. I steadied him on his bed and ran my hand through his hair, trying to keep my voice even. "You mean there's a replica of Hercermer in heaven?"

**Also something that will be in your mansion were the sandals holding your feet as Medea in that play with Dad. You liked those sandals, and you wore them on stage. Holy workers stirred the other grandma to make them for you. The sandals worn when you started to date my dad. It was a fun nudge for him to be your mate, so you will have sandals there.**

*Somebody please pick my jaw off the floor.* We'd never told him *any* of these things. He certainly didn't know that in my senior year in college, I'd worn a pair of Greek-looking crisscross leather shoes that tied at the ankles. They could have passed for something Jesus wore, but they were perfect for my production and had always held special meaning to me. So he knew about that too? I watched with rapt interest to see what else he knew.

**I love my mansion. It is big and it has my piano in it. My planted fingers plunk it out with music like plain pianos have never heard. It is designed like you're inside, but it is not hurting your ears at all. Will it say I'm lighting up a piano one day on earth? It means this to me.**

**Going for my mansion built up joy like I'd never felt, to see huge monkey bars in my own house.**

**My greatest part is this light on the ceiling. It is thought to be a big mighty chandelier, but it is not. It is my joyful paper I**

have written, as if it is inside of the chandelier lighting up joy in my life.

Part of my own mansion has built into it furniture I love to ascend to highest heights by jumping on.

Josiah leaped to his feet and started jumping on his bed. "Hey, what are you doing?" I said. "Trying to give me a demonstration? Excuse me, but we aren't in heaven yet and I don't think your mattress can take it, so please stop." Laughing, I grabbed him around the middle and reined him in beside me.

My furniture is so springy, it fails me to answer as to how high the ceiling even is. My home is not quite ready, but it is mine. It houses my life so far. Like I'm its designer, only I'm not.

Always I see mansions. I just see inside mine and some of yours and basically, it is not ok for me to tell you anymore than about Hercermer and your sandals you loved. I only see the outside. It is all quite different in their looks and their kinds. It is like the person. Your mansion is added to as you grow and love things in your heavenly places.

Josiah bit the edge of his bedspread. I silently thanked God for him and his out-of-this-world experiences. Then I dashed to my room to call my mom.

"You'll never believe this." And I shared Josiah's latest.

She sighed. "Oh, Tahni, he's seen our relatives. They're closer than we know. Josiah's right about the beds too. I'd completely forgotten about them, but it's absolutely true. Your dad turned Matthew and Mandy's bunk beds into a crib."

"Why?" I asked.

"Oh, I don't know. Probably because you told us that Hercermer needed the bed to have sides so he wouldn't fall out."

I laughed. "I didn't mean that. I meant why is all this happening to our family?"

"I don't know," she said. "But I think we need to keep trusting God and thanking him for all these awesome revelations. Who knows, maybe someday he will even show us a few of the wonderful purposes behind them."

# 25

# Trial the Truth

"Jesus took a lopsided nail
to open up a lopsided love."

– Josiah Cullen

**Summer 2014**

Josiah stood in front of the sink naked like an unmovable stone statue. **Tell me to go in the shower,** he typed.

"Fine. Go in the shower." The instant I pulled back the curtain, however, he ran from me. "Hey, stop! It is *so* frustrating when you say one thing and do another."

A couple of hours later, I sat with him on the couch, wishing I could start the whole week over. The air conditioner, the car, everything seemed to be breaking down in the Cullen household. But Josiah's behavior irked me more than anything—and on my birthday, no less.

"What's on your mind, big guy?"

**Worry is not my portion, Mom, to bear. So, historically, worry is totally worth nothing under the sun and the Son.**

**Voice that worry is not your negative friend. It is the music that makes the discordant note that stops the opus dead in its tracks. Would it hire the major trials to be your focus? It would. So make a mountain go, or it will stop your song.**

**Now post it on Facebook.**

Three days later, he wiggled his butt on the couch and typed another mind-bender.

**Trials are to truth, not to suffering. So it is tuned to hurry truth to you. Not to hurt you, but to hurry you to see the truth faster than you otherwise would.**

**A trial is the tuning of your soul to voice life to realities that demand change.**

**Jesus says, "Trial the truth of body broken, of blood spilled. Make truth meet the standard truth: it is finished."**

**The world is trialed now only by the truth. Break, taste, drink, see that the truth is so good. Trials are to truth, not to suffering.**

I had to read it over and over. My goodness, this had come from my unruly son who had to struggle his way in the shower? He was absolutely right! The trial wasn't my financial woes, my crazy life, or anything else. The trial was whether or not I believed God's truth. Did I believe the Lord when he said he'd supply all my needs according to his riches in glory? Did I believe my God who spoke the world into existence and loved me even before I was born?

At the end of the week, Josiah was up and raring to go. **Take me somewhere where there's music**, he typed. Thankfully, I knew just the place. The Irish Festival.

When we arrived, Josiah moved his body to the beat of the fiddles, flutes, accordions, and hand drums. Dancers spun, feet kicked, skirts flared, and children laughed. As we passed booths with goodies and activities, Josiah looked like a little Irishman in his flat cap and Ireland T-shirt. Joe's Irish parents would have been proud.

We passed men in kilts puffing their cheeks into bagpipes. Fair-skinned dancer girls rushing around in wigs with bouncy curls reminded me of my mom's dolls.

I gave Josiah's hand a light squeeze and swung it back and forth, then gave him a twirl that earned me a laugh.

"Hey, JoJo, look at the Irish dogs. Setters, terriers, sheepdogs.

I wonder how many little hands will pet them over the next few days."

We passed baked goods in the food tent, and I bought Josiah a cinnamon scone. We poked around vendor tables in the market-place tent, eyeballing jewelry, sports jerseys, leather journals, Celtic crosses, Irish outfits for dogs, and scarves and hats of all kinds.

"Try on a hat?" the salesman asked.

"Why not," I said. I slapped it on and angled myself in front of the mirror. "What do you think, JoJo? Oh, you look flushed. Let's go outside by the water."

We wound our way past the white-topped tents and took the sidewalk along the banks of the Mississippi.

"Look, JoJo. Check out the St. Paul skyscrapers on the other side. Hey, wait! Stop! Don't get too close to the rail." It wouldn't have been the first time he sent his cap and glasses for a swim, but I especially didn't want him to join them.

As we walked hand in hand, I thought about my family's recent reunion in the Black Hills of South Dakota. Josiah had experienced his first reunion there, and just a month later, he'd spiraled into autism.

Strangely, at the recent reunion, Josiah wanted to tell my cousin Talitha about Mary and Rusty's kids and their families. He couldn't stop sharing about the value of family and how much he cherished it. As he typed, his eyes actually filled with tears.

**Josiah is like a real boy. I want to talk and bond with Talitha. Rolling tears are my way of saying to the kin of Rusty and Mary that we are kissing heaven right now. Let me say I am so happy. Like faith is poetry. It is all circular.**

Joe and I had marveled that he felt such a close connection with our extended families when we hadn't even spent much time with them.

With a light heart from Josiah's sensitivities, the two of us cut back across the grass and worked our way to the big white canopy for the dance competitions.

Perfect—two seats at the end of a row! We sat down, and the girls on the stage began to twirl. Josiah reached into my purse for the iPad and leaned his pointy elbow on my leg.

**A lineage of Irish joy. The picture is so lovely. I've basically written it already in my mind. I tell you, I'm liking it so much.**

His body rocked to the taps of the girls' feet.

**Send God's love to the Irish tribe**
**Bless the maid, bless the man**
**Move the feet, move the hands**
**Timid, listening arms stay still**
**Like furious, listening arms they are**
**Arms blessed by stillness**
**While legs fastly spare no time**
**To heal the land**
**It is true, the dance heals the land**
**Rich it is to dance like a child of the king**
**Furious, yet originating from joy**
**It is like dangerous hindsight**
**That hastens the wind of the holy one**
**To blow into town**

Just then, a gust of wind blew through, rippling the canvas of the canopy.

**Triune delights shake this rich place**
**I am not only a boy**
**I am an Irish boy, rich in my heritage**
**Raise your spirits, brothers and lasses**
**Trials come and go**
**It is your inheritance, little children**
**To hire the dance**
**To hire the little band**
**To hire the little clackers**
**To be your blessed maker's tools**
**That is your joy**

His words made me imagine every culture and tribe, equally and distinctly loved by their Master, dancing around the throne.

We stepped outside and walked to the back of the stage where clusters of outfitted girls waited to be called to the platform. Just then, someone on the other side of the tent caught my eye: a severely disabled woman in her thirties. She sat by herself in a wheelchair with a computer mounted in front of her contorted body.

I sauntered over. "Hi, I'm Tahni and this is my son, Josiah."

Her face lit up, but her body tensed, and she shook as she tried to speak. Oh no. I'd gotten her all riled up and over-stimulated. I considered making a quick escape, but a mechanical voice spoke from a machine. "My name is Siabon."

"Oh." I tried to hide my surprise. "Hi, Siabon. I see you have a screen in front of your wheelchair. My son Josiah here has autism and uses a special app to type with an iPad. How do you use your screen when your hands aren't moving?"

"I control the machine with my eyes," said the mechanical voice.

"Wow, I've never seen that before." I cleared my throat. "Are you enjoying the festival?"

"I love it," she said. "I'm Irish. Are you?"

I noticed a small reflective dot on her forehead and realized it probably had a sensor that connected to the keyboard in front of her.

"A little Irish," I said. "But Josiah here is very Irish. His last name is Cullen."

I looked from her face to the screen, and she broke into staccato outbursts. Josiah stayed so detached in his world that I couldn't even tell if he'd paid attention to our conversation.

At one thirty the next morning, he went on a writing spree.

"Can't this wait?" I said, sounding cranky as I flopped on the couch.

**This rising is to tell you to hire the mysterious truth. The truth is to do what is said or it isn't true. So it is with God like that.**

**The truth is true only if it follows through. God must do what he has said, or he is mundane like your son to say one thing and do another. Trial this truth. He says, "I am truth and I am true too."**

His words hit a tender spot. It was one thing to trust God about myself, quite another to trust him with my own son. The dam broke and the sobs ripped out.

*I don't get it, God. How can Josiah be in the presence of you and your angels and not be all the way healed? You say you are truth and true. Well, in that case, when are you going to truly heal him?*

Josiah's finger went wild. **The sound is your Socrates trying to work it out to say, "Well, if I don't see it, sound it, or yield it, it isn't happening." Not so. His voice comes, so Tahni, hold on. His voice comes.**

**So your rich sobs show that you break to say, "I don't see Jesus working this out. It looks so bad right now. My son is so autistic. He is richly worse than he has ever been when it comes to his real self showing through." Right?**

I wiped my eyes. "Josiah, what am I supposed to say?"

**Holy tears though, you cry. Holy tears to say what you believe has to become true, or it is only half true. Only delight in me, and I will do all I have said to you. He is walking out of autism, Tahni. I am the first and the last. So he will speak. Like a real boy. Not on a machine like the lady you saw. Picturing that maybe he could do that with his eyes one day.**

**So hard to believe for her to be healed, right? I am seeing it now. You wanted her to be whole, right? So do I, Tahni. So do I.**

**Hasten this day to voice that you will see this richly all over the world. She is afflicted by infirmity. So you raise her up boldly to say, "Be healed, bright one." And to say that you are not worth joy would be to say that you are not worth as much as a sparrow. So proudly say, "Walk straight. Straighten her up."**

**I want you to say, "Limits off this body, in Jesus' name."**

**Sorry, Mom. The worker says—the voice is so strong—to voice, "Limits off, in Jesus' name."**

**Holy is this word of my Jesus to you, Mom. I am sure you will be spiritually shown what happens with limits off in the Bible. Trial the truth now.**

*Breathe*, I told myself. Honestly, it would have been easier to accept things the way they were. At least I wouldn't have to keep setting myself up for more disappointment. On the other hand, how could I accept our current ugly situation when God kept speaking to me through our miracle boy about miracles?

*Healing God, you say, "All things are possible." Please tell me again this includes everything from you healing the effects of autism to you straightening out a woman in a wheelchair.*

*If this is my trial for the truth—that you do what you say and you never change—dear God, I ask you help me believe it.*

## 26

# Kid Stuff

"Worship God with laughter."

– Josiah Cullen

**Summer 2014**

Like most sporty dads, Joe dreamed of tossing around a ball with his son and venturing to Little League games. Josiah couldn't do these things, but at least he could join a T-ball group for kids with special needs. Some played in wheelchairs while others couldn't focus enough or get themselves coordinated, but Joe didn't let any of this bother him. He simply loved supporting his boy.

Joe had spent his first nine years in New York, which meant his dad used to take him to watch the Mets. So guess who played against the Minnesota Twins for Josiah's first game?

"Go Mets!" Joe shouted.

He and Josiah looked like twins in their matching Mets shirts while I cheered for the Twins in my Twins shirt. As we passionately cheered for opposing teams, we hid our hyper selves in the far back row. Whenever Josiah became antsy, I'd walk with him somewhere.

"What do you say we go to the concession and buy you a toy?"

Josiah knew he could have anything, but he picked a loofah, one of those hanging shower sponges. This one came attached to a plush blue bear, the Twins' mascot. Returning to our seats, I developed a special fondness for this blue loofah bear. He saved the day by keeping Josiah in his chair until the seventh inning.

When Joe's parents came to town, we wanted them to share in our newfound fun, so we invited them to join Josiah at his second Twins game.

Something about this particular game brought out Josiah's adventurous side. When a child has autism, food is always a major big deal. Children with autism are often hesitant to try new things. So when Josiah wrote that he wanted to try popcorn, we all sat on the edge of our seats. Sure enough, he gobbled down several big handfuls.

"What did you think of it, JoJo?"

He pulled us away to a quiet nook and began to type.

**Call tasty popcorn my worries over that rich blasts in my hot natural desire will besiege my joys. First time I put a piece in my mouth, it was rammed in there.**

**The next time, it was hesitantly put in there, hoping I was not mistaken that it was good—like a rat IDs a cheese on a trap. It was not a trap! Richly I ate another piece. Boy, was it a job well done.**

**I had attitudinally worked myself into a frenzy over popcorn. I am doubting that basic approach altogether now.**

Goodness, how did that boy even manage to turn popcorn into a life lesson? On the drive home, we all felt thankful for a homerun day.

One day, when I went to Michaels to stock up on washable paints, Josiah had a plan of his own. While I looked one way down the aisle, Josiah, who sat in my cart looking fairly innocent, began to load up our cart with squishy toys.

"Nice caterpillars," I said when I caught him. "You're funny, and since you're also so cute, I'll let you pick one to buy. Which one do you want?" I held up my iPad and steadied his hand.

**So many worms will have to rapidly worm out of my worm collection. Random sale! I get three.**

I cleared my throat. "Ahem. You get one."

**I am trialed now. Which one to get? I say all the worms want to come with me.**

"You can have one," I repeated. "What color would you like?"

**Is it a mark of hard labor to get two?**

"No, tonight you'll be happy with one. Tell you what. I'll let you get two, but that's it. What colors do you want?"

Josiah clawed through the bin and sorted them by color.

**Joy. There are so many original squishy worms. I want orange and yellow. Okay. It would be good to put the rest back like a delightful boy.**

"You're right," I said. "That *would* be delightful."

**It is so hard. It's like the worms are clapping for my worm pass to get out of here. It is like daily they worm about only to never leave that bin. It's so hard to be a worm here. The worms say, "Please take us all."**

"Sorry," I said. "I'm sure there will be other little boys and girls who can adopt them. You get two."

Josiah cocked his head and plunked down his finger. **I guess I will take the orange and yellow. The other worms want to stay with me, but they can't. Actually, Josiah will spare the yellow and green one. Oh, random sale! I get three.**

"No," I said. "You get two."

**I am rich. I have the money.**

"Oh, really? You have money?"

**You should work harder.**

"That's nice." I tried to suppress a laugh.

**I will have to voice a sobering goodbye to my worms now.** But even after saying that, he snuck in another attempt. **Spare my worms, please!**

"You don't give up easily, do you?" I smiled at a couple of older ladies. "Seriously," I said, "you get two. You need to choose now."

**Hard choice.** Then he tried another tactic. He wrote on behalf of the worms. **Spare me, Tahni. Slink, slink. I want to come with you too.**

He clicked his tongue and made a high-pitched sound. **I would really be glad to have three.**

"And you'll also be glad to have two. That is my final generous offer."

Josiah gave the caterpillars one last sad woeful look, then wrote his farewell. **Worms, you try to stay, but Mom says no. Voice my loss to be your dad. Like ants to blackness, you will return. I'm so sorry.**

I couldn't help myself, I burst out laughing. I'd always known he was a charmer, but this was his first negotiation.

"Good thing I'm not a pushover," I said, watching his fingers fumble in the bin and grab two new colors. "Now come on." I pushed him to the checkout, where I unloaded the cart and paid for our new pets. "It's official, JoJo. You are now the proud owner of your very own orange and pink worms."

## 27

# Sound of Music

"Music is my song for what I did to redeem the world.
It is from me, to me, through me. I am the fullness of music,
so I am the sound I want coming from my church."

– Josiah Cullen

**Summer 2014**

"Tahni, your son is rocking my world."

I gripped the steering wheel with one hand and held my cell phone with the other. What a surprise to hear from Mark Bierle, the guy I used to talk to about Josiah when I worked at Eagle Brook. Mark had been inspired by how technology gave Josiah a voice, and as a result, he wanted to donate iPads for the kids at the church with special needs. We'd chitchatted a bit since then, but we didn't really know each other that well. His interest in Josiah's Facebook page, however, had recently changed all that.

"Mark," I said, "you don't even know the half of it."

He cleared his throat. "I'm sure you're dealing with a lot, but I want you to know that God used your son to give me a double confirmation. God's using him to speak in a big way, and my ears are wide open."

A few days later, I received a similar word of encouragement from Scott Sample, another man from church. This time it came in the form of a Facebook message. Scott was an amazing artist, and sometimes when I passed him in the church lobby near his large paintings that hung on the wall, I'd thank him for sharing his gift.

I'd met his wife, Stephanie, years before at a woman's event. She shared with us all how God sustained them through the loss of their ten-month-old son in a daycare accident. Then Stephanie came to hear me speak at a fall retreat. That's when she learned about Josiah and started following his Facebook page. I loved the story she shared about her conversation with her husband.

"Who do you think wrote this?" she asked Scott.

"I don't know," he said. "Brennan Manning?"

"No. Josiah Cullen, a little eight-year-old boy with autism."

As soon as Scott discovered Josiah, he followed his Facebook posts and liked them so much that he messaged me after he misplaced one.

"Uh … what was it about?" I asked.

"It was the one where Josiah talks about the failing of worship."

I knew exactly the one. It came embedded in a list, so I sent Scott the whole thing:

**Jesus says spirituality is quite a little issue down there, and the triune God would like to single out some problems.**

**1. Turning to use dear troubles only as a pity party is an issue. Call it joy when you are faced with trials. It is proving that faith works. It is trials that position faith to work. It is problematic to hint at bondage and never try to break the bondage.**

**2. Spill the beans. It is ignorant to tempt the nearly stinginess of Americans. It is judgment not to care for another's mother or father. Trouble your wallets and sponsor an elderly person today. It is probably the most overlooked group in America.**

**Stir up money for elderly people and pray with them. It is pride that joylessly leaves them to fend for themselves. It is pride that joylessly pictures them as lowly and out of touch. They are a lineage of bondages broken and bondages born. Pots of love need to go to elders today.**

3. Laughter is a problem. Is it hard to laugh, truly laugh? Just plow a driveway and tons of people are grumpy all day long. Get over it. Lucky you are to have a house. People, it's time to laugh!

Businesses trouble themselves to smile at people. It is funny that my people don't stop and stare in someone's eyes, and laugh, noting a nice shirt or scarf. It is luscious to name a nice quality in someone. Do it often, my people. It is laughs and troubles lifted. It is nice to do this, people!

4. Jot it down! Stories of spine-tingling miracles need to be told much more. How about I start healing kids who taste nudges to line things up, and listen badly, and speak sparingly, and you start talking about it, giving natural praise to me?

It is the like mission of this kid to rile up the world. It is proud Papa God that lines it all up, rotely troubling dumb mouths to speak, truly telling them to speak, and they will speak!

5. Treat one another with "lean-in love." Truly lean in! Get hockey sticks out of your spines and hug each other! It isn't that hard, people. Dunces know how to hug better than my people. Con artists hug better than my people.

6. Rise up music to me that positively answers my question, "Do you love me?" Feed my sheep. It is only singers, not worshipers, that sputter intelligent words but live like they don't care a thing about proudly, proudly praising me.

It is rotten to slog through minors and skip the majors time and again. Pockets of double-minded choices about how to sing something are missing the point. How about just answering the question, "Do you love me?" Don't worry if it's catchy. Just worry if it's sung with passion and truth. It is like a gong to me if it is clever, but not joyful or stirring to the spirit of God's breath on you. Jot it down, musicians, and I'll bend my ear to nurture your congregation.

*That's it,* Scott wrote. *Thank you!*

I didn't mention a thing about our exchange to Josiah. I didn't even mention Scott's name, but Josiah knew. Not only that, but he also had a personal message just for Scott.

Poet is mostly saying that so claused is g that, spiritually, worship sort of muses to end on g. The king doesn't pocket it as the most joyful use of musicians to hit g, for it is a lonely sounding note. It is long overdue to hit us with lots of new pints of little jars of ale to hit unusual music. Little classic love songs are delightful to me. I am now picking faithful, mature, delightful man Scott Sample to hire faithful, delightful man from the east to praise mostly originally with abcdef, not g.

Scott wrote back, amazed. *That reference to G has been a solid metaphor I have used over and over. It's very specific to G and ending on G. You and Josiah could never know that except from the Father. Now that is crazy business.*

Josiah's word impacted Scott so much that he asked if I'd send him any older words on worship, so I did.

Worship studies your bangles to ring like walking with a jingle. To voice joy is to voice full life in my Son.

Luscious qualms about laughter in church are funny to me. I am not unpleased with laughter—ever. It is the music of laughter that muses on my worthy love, muses on my sandy beaches' tremendous, worthy rain.

To have fun is to have my poetry working to hide truth in your stirring to listen.

To run to love this way spoils the music of my fussy, fussy adversary. Would Satan laugh? Only to hide his terror of the power stirring in my students of guaranteed love.

Move fun to hasten your kisses from not only stories turning the pages but stories—lots of stories—of turning the nurture of negativity on its listening ear.

Sturdy, tangible laughter loves turning from language of martyr to language of victor.

Scott replied, *Wow, wow, wow. Let's just say it was the first time I had tears in my eyes while in a Jiffy Lube. What really nailed me was that the "laughter" aspect of our faith has been sooo missing for way too long. It has really been on my heart, and Josiah has a gift for nailing truth. Once again, God's timing is beautiful.*

I then learned that Mark ran into Scott, and the two of them discovered they'd both been contacting me about Josiah—around the same time. Their mutual interest in my son led them to contact their friend who happened to be a Grammy award-winning musician.

I never would have expected to find myself sitting at the Lobster Smack Shack around a table with Scott, Mark, and their friend, but that's exactly what happened. This well-known producer, singer, songwriter from Nashville looked at me with sincerity and told me he was "blown away" by Josiah.

I set down my water and beamed. "This is such an honor."

"Likewise," he said. "These guys have told me a lot of amazing things about Josiah."

Scott nodded. "God is radically using that boy, and I love his words about music. As you all know, I've been sensing God wants to do something new and different with worship and the arts. Musicians spend gobs of time chasing what the culture is doing. There just has to be another way. Wouldn't it be great if we could create music, art, and worship that's new and unique? Worship that flows right out of our passion for God?"

"That lines up with Josiah's words," I said. "He writes about God wanting music to awaken the world to say, 'What's that sound?' Kind of like the music revolution of the 1950s when new sounds emerged. It captured the creative imagination of a culture."

Even as I said it, I felt an ache to reflect that same kind of a sound back to the Father. A sound that would join angels in what Josiah called "a holy tremble."

"Wouldn't it be incredible," Scott said, "to see speakers, musicians, artists, dancers, and film makers get together in a non-churchy venue to worship in a way that answered God's question, 'Do you love me?'"

We all nodded in agreement, and Scott continued.

"I just came across a C. S. Lewis book called *Letters to Malcolm*. This is wild, but I randomly flipped to a page where Lewis wrote about worship. He mentioned how thinking about worship is different from actually worshiping. Listen to this." He pulled up the page on his iPad. "I wish that they'd remember that the charge to Peter was 'If you love me, feed my sheep.'" Scott paused. "That line was such a confirmation to Josiah's word from the Lord. I'm telling you, it's changing my direction."

I breathed in the smell of fresh-baked bread and seafood and then exhaled. I might not have had a musical bone in my body, but I knew the sound of the Spirit had precisely drawn the four of us together, and once again the Father had used my son to be a blessing.

"Josiah always keeps teaching me things," I said. "He showed me that when Jesus lived on earth, he broke all standard social conventions. I wrote a talk called *Mary of Bethany*. It's interesting because Mary, the sister of Martha and Lazarus, shows up several times in Scripture. We see her fearless devotion. She sat at Jesus' feet at a time in history when only the disciples of the rabbis did that. And certainly a woman would never dare. Men were supposed to keep at least six feet away from them, but Mary hungered to learn from him, just like she desired to bless and anoint him.

"God showed me that Mary didn't just want to 'do devotions.' She wanted to *be* devoted to him. She worshiped him in spirit and truth.

"If you want, I can send you the whole talk. It's funny because when I was writing it, I didn't tell Josiah I was struggling to come up with an ending. I didn't have to because he said, 'God wants to give you the ending for your Mary talk.' And so he did."

The guys shook their heads, amazed, and Scott spoke up.

"All I can say is that Steph and I have been profoundly affected by Josiah's personal words to us. They're almost like psalmist language. I take time to artfully diagram them so I can revisit them.

I've even started writing a book because of one of them. They encourage me to press in and hear God's voice, and I've come to realize I'm not crazy. God really does want to talk to me about what's on his heart."

When I returned home, their words worked themselves over in my mind. My autistic son kept dishing up truth that helped people from a wide range of backgrounds be able to look at life differently. I hadn't prayed for this or even wanted it, but it stretched me as much as it did anyone else.

It also expanded my taste in music. I used to see the old hymns as outdated, but now I saw them as timeless powerful declarations designed to draw a whole culture to the Holy Spirit. I also loved to raise my antennae to fresh springs of worship that flowed from God's heart, wooing me closer.

Josiah's words had transformed Mark and Scott's view of worship, but they had clearly changed my perspective as well. Whenever I released worshipful sounds and words, they released me too. Rather than tossing songs to a distant God, I started to sing as if Jesus was standing right in front of me. Like we were the only ones in the room. My home became his throne room, and I would bow, dance, and cry in his presence.

*Father, we're growing closer. I can feel it.*

I felt so smitten as heaven's sounds swirled in my head. I could only imagine what kind of tunes the Creator of music would release into my life next.

## 28

# All about Love

"Jesus is safely in you, and lots of angels
order your gates to open up around you
in order to join to others who need love."

– Josiah Cullen

**Fall 2014**

As I stood in Mom's new store I fingered cross necklaces on the front rack. I could hardly believe I had actually flown to Washington State and was now standing in the prophesied Peace Café.

With financial backing from my aunt and cousin, my mom claimed a place on the north side of Main Street. On May 25, Peace Café opened to the public. Mom sold inspirational gifts like jewelry, art, signs, wooden home décor, and plaques with Josiah's sayings. In the food section at the back, she sold soup, homemade buns, snickerdoodle cookies, and of course, coffee with all the fixings. Josiah had basically laid out the whole menu and Mom had followed it.

I still found it hard to believe that my almost-seventy-year-old mother had stepped out of retirement to jump into this walloping "apple dare." It was one thing to make dolls from scraps, quite another to build a store from scratch. And so much more than a store. A marketplace ministry. A sacrifice.

The week before Mom planned to open it, my aunt had a

serious stroke that weakened her left side. Mom and her friends marched right into that nursing home, praying and declaring, "You will live and not die. You will one day walk through the doors of Peace Café."

They were right. I felt thrust in a dream as I stood in the store watching that same aunt laugh it up with Mom's customers.

Coffee smells from the espresso machine drew me to the other side of the room. There I glanced at the *Open House* sign on the door and inhaled the savory smell of simmering soups.

Amid the buzz of excitement, however, I felt a tinge of nervousness. How could my mom keep up with all this? Clearly, she must have trusted God more than I did.

A local church group set up their guitars, drums, and keyboard for a gig. In just a few hours, I'd be standing in that same spot to publicly talk about God, the good gift giver. I laughed, because I could say anything I wanted and the owner wouldn't throw me out. Seriously though, I had a story to tell, a miracle story. I couldn't think of a better place to tell it than smack in the middle of the prophesied Peace Café.

More guests stepped inside, and I hustled from the back to the gift area in the front. Just then a middle-aged woman looked my way, and I smiled warmly. "Welcome to our fall open house. Have you been to Peace Café before?"

"No. First time." She ran a hand through her hair. "I've walked by, but I finally decided to come check it out."

"Well, I'm glad you did. Hey, I like your walking stick. It kind of reminds me of the willow branch cane my grandfather used to use."

"It keeps me standing." She lowered herself onto a chair at a table. "I just had knee surgery for the second time."

"Oh, that doesn't sound like fun."

"No, it's been one rough thing after the other. My apartment just flooded. Who knows what will happen next."

"Oh no. Sorry to hear about your apartment. Can we help you with that? Maybe loan you our shop vacuum or something?"

"No, thanks. They're already working on it." She rubbed her temples. "I haven't even told you the worst of it. My fifty-two-year-old husband recently had a brain aneurysm, so I had to put him in a nursing home. Now my stepkids will hardly talk to me."

God's compassion stirred inside. "So sorry to hear about that. That's a lot to deal with."

"Oh, you have no idea."

"You're right, I don't. My name's Tahni, by the way. What's yours?"

"Elaine."

"Elaine, would you mind if I prayed for you?"

She jerked back. "Listen, I respect your beliefs and everything, but no, thank you."

"That's fine. I understand."

She stepped to the counter and bought clam chowder and a sandwich. When she sat back down, I listened to her heart until she didn't have anything left to say.

"I'm not going to pray for you in the traditional sense," I said. "But I do want you to know there will be better days ahead. And you know what? The God who formed you cares about your pain and tears. You're a beautiful person. I have a son with severe autism, so I know a bit about pain—but I've also found hope."

Traces of hardness melted off her face. "I was raised in the church," she said. "But after all these horrible things happened to me, I became an atheist or agnostic, whatever you want to call it." She grew quiet, then leaned in. "You know what? If I did believe in a God, I'd think I was looking at him right now. I see him in your eyes."

"Oh, thank you so much." I gave her a hug.

When I returned to my mom's house, I collapsed on my bed, weary but fulfilled. Forty-five people had stopped at the store for my mini speaking engagement. I hadn't expected that many, and several had tears. I'd hoped Elaine would stay, but at least I'd given her a solid hour of my time.

Just then, I remembered the sealed card I'd shoved in my purse after one of Mom's employees handed it to me.

I opened the envelope to a colorful card from Peace Café with Elaine's name printed neatly at the bottom. She must have asked the employee to give to me. My heart leaped as I read her note.

*You didn't know this, but I was feeling suicidal today and you talked to me for a lengthy time. I began to dare to hope, and now as I leave this store several hours later, I am daring to live, smile, and be me.*

*Thank you,*
*Elaine R.*

Tears filled my eyes. *Okay, God. I'm officially undone. You've wrecked me. It boggles me how you even work with broken people like me. What can I say? Thank you for caring enough to reach across the room and save a life.*

When I returned home four days later, it became clear that Josiah had been moved by an apple dare.

**Take hamburgers to homeless people, will you?**
**It's not that hard or that expensive.**
**For it is like a drop in most people's bucket.**
**You prize the food yourself and they would too.**
**Hide happiness toward them in a blessing to say,**
**"You are seen by Jesus and he sent me.**
**Black and white, red and yellow, he sends me to you.**
**Trade the farthest sadness for his holy world's hope.**
**Face the day to present yourself to him, asking for his help.**
**He is trialed by your pain.**
**He is sorry for your sadness."**
**Just make it like this: feed the one in front of you.**
**Tell them, "Jesus sees you," that is enough.**
**He is the real phenomenal Savior.**
**Holy is the barn that keeps fives on them to give away.**
**So do this to many to help them live with hope again.**

**To say you made them see love.**
**Hand them hamburgers and a five.**


The next day, I went to McDonald's, bought eight hamburgers and turned a twenty-dollar bill into fives. Then I loaded the bags with the cash.

*Okay, Lord. Let's go somewhere and be a blessing.*

I drove to a place where people normally held signs, but nobody was there.

*Oh no. Where are the signs, Lord?*

Fighting disappointment, I drove to an unfamiliar area where a woman stood on a corner holding a Little Caesar's Pizza marketing sign. This wasn't exactly what I had in mind when I said *signs*.

*You're funny, God.*

I looked more closely at the woman and noticed her shabby coat, ragged hat, and the grungy bag propped against a pole. How had she ever passed the job interview? Had the managers hired her out of kindness? Perhaps they wanted to help a homeless woman earn some extra cash.

I circled the block, arguing with God. *Whoever heard of giving a McDonald's burger to a Little Caesar's employee? People just don't do that. What if her boss gives her trouble, and I end up making things worse?*

Finally, I pulled over and rolled down my window.

"Hi. This might sound funny, but … are you hungry? Because if you are, I have some burgers if you'd like."

"Are you kidding?" she said. "I'd love one. Thanks so much!"

"Here you go, hon." I handed her the bag and added what Josiah told me to say. "I just want you to know that God sees you. Have a blessed day."

Joy swept over me as I drove off. *We did it, Lord. In your power, you used a little burger to deliver big hope.*

Energized, I drove to another popular homeless spot, but there I ran into the same problem. Where were the people? My stomach rumbled, and I felt tired. This ministry of driving around looking for hungry people took a lot out of a girl. *Perhaps I should just go home*, I thought. *Give the rest of the food to Joe and Josiah and call it a day.*

But just as I drove toward the ramp, I saw a guy on the other side of the interstate holding a sign. A real bona fide person in need. Yes! But in order to reach him, I'd have to circle around, exit the ramp at just the right time, get a red light, and be able to stop fairly close. Otherwise, the light could turn green, and I'd have to keep going.

*Okay, Father. If you want this to happen, you're going to have to put everything in place.*

I circled around, and bam—the light turned red right when I needed it to. I came to a stop with just two cars in front of me. *Thank you, Lord.* Rolling down my window, I waved the man over. "Want some burgers?" I hollered.

His face wrinkled into a smile beneath his well-worn veteran's hat. "Thank you, ma'am. God bless."

"He already is," I said, handing him the bag. "He sees you and cares about you."

I felt his penetrating eyes stare after me as I drove off. Then came the doubts. What if he used the money to buy booze or drugs?

*Stop*, I told myself. *Don't be silly. God's in control, not you. Just love the people and trust God with the rest.*

Trust had this funny way of sounding so much easier in theory than it did in practice. It frightened me every time I stepped out and faced possible rejection and failure. But this trust test was nothing compared to how God wanted me to lay down my son on his altar.

Sadly, something told me I still wasn't quite there yet.

## 29

# Work It Out

"Tell them that Father is nice. It is Papa boasting
in you because you let him help you—no other reason."

– Josiah Cullen

**September 2014**

I stood in front of four hundred women during the Minnesota Baptist General Conference at Trout Lake Camp. Hopefully this topic of "Making Things New" would make a life-changing difference in their hearts. Who didn't face life's battles on a daily basis and need some kind of repair and restoration?

God's promises had been leaping off the page for me lately, particularly his vow to care for us through every season.

After I finished speaking, women rushed over to share how much they'd been challenged or changed by something I said. Wasn't that just like the Lord to speak so intimately and individually to so many people at once?

Josiah understood this kind of personal intimacy with the Lord. His relationship with God continued to challenge me and ignite my hunger for more.

Sometimes after pouring out myself on my family and others, I'd retreat to my room and look back on Josiah's words. Not only did they reveal his profound understanding of the Lord's goodness and favor, but they also reminded me that even in life's toughest seasons, the Father's presence and voice in Josiah's life could work maturity in him in a way that surpassed even our best efforts and abilities.

**I interact with my huge Papa in little chats one-on-one about my aging into a man of daring future might. He tells me things I'm to know, but I'm just so joyful to milk long at his dear safe chest. I'm just loved so much in his very kind arms.**

**Jesus votes in favor of me. He gets me. He notes my areas of basic struggles, because he knows them. I'm not holding anything from him, because he is nice to put our trust in him.**

On October 4, 2014, my baby turned nine. I'd always dreaded Josiah's birthdays for all the hope they did not deliver. While we ached for notable progress, birthdays spoke loud and clear of the ever-widening gap in our constant quest for some semblance of normalcy.

Even gift shopping jostled my spirits. In Toys "R" Us, I'd pass elaborate Lego sets and superhero action toys. I'd have to park my cart in the toddler section, where I'd test out all those beeping toys with their push-button noises that made me want to scream in protest.

This birthday felt different though. I felt more joy and a lot less fear. God's presence had become almost tangible, and he'd shown me that with him I could handle more than I thought. After all, he'd helped me handle Josiah.

To celebrate his birthday, Joe and I took Josiah to his first indoor concert, *Disney Live!* at the Target Center. I slipped my arm around Josiah's shoulder. "Hey, look. There's Belle and the Beast."

During intermission I pulled out the iPad. "What do you think about the music?"

**Music is fun that you feel.**

I laughed. "You're right. It is."

Scott Sample gave us a family gift, a striking painting of an angel ablaze with light and color. We placed the glory-being close to our couch, the perfect place since we spent so much time there.

Josiah noticed the painting and began to type. **Show me art, and I will show you a muse. Show me ideas, and I will show you a muse. Show me a daring, far-reaching plan, and I will show you a muse.**

**Desire fast angels to help you do things today, for they are so great to have on your side.**

"Incredible, awesome, amazing," I said. "I am glad they're for us. Hey, JoJo. I've been thinking on something you said about angels in training. What exactly did you mean by that? I imagine people like us are in training—but angels? How does that work?"

**Angels will be judged. How? On their hardships? On their building blocks? On their hurrying? It is based on their might in serving us.**

**Might is bigger than loud leadership. You thought leaders were honored by their ranking. In heaven, they are honored by their might within their lighting up of their purpose. Life is supposed to be like this.**

**You are in training if major angel of might notes you are careful to press in making banter with your huge human, or not nudging enough, or not moving to language best might to them. It is big to know this. It is might, not rank, that makes an angel honored in heaven.**

*Lord, help me light up for you.* I squinted at the painting and let its color swim into my vision. As I thought about the importance of stepping into my purpose, Josiah took his pointer finger and pounded out a prayer.

**Father, make my work so it is loudly sung to history. Stir it up, oh great God. Make me dust it off, get it used. I am listening for your story to sing over me. Solve every missing link.**

My stomach fluttered one cold November night as I hustled down the hall for my first parent-teacher conference of the year. I thought about Josiah's "stirred up body," and prayed a quick popcorn prayer for Joe who'd stayed home to watch him. I rushed past the regular lockers and classrooms until I hit the far back corner where two small autism classrooms lay tucked away.

Josiah's teacher and occupational therapist stood to shake my hand before I joined them at a tiny kid table on a super-small chair.

"What happened?" I said, pointing to the teacher's walking boot.

"I broke my pinky toe."

"Ouch," I said.

I glanced around the room at the hodge-podge of activity centers. *Boy*, I thought. *This place would be distracting for Josiah.*

"How's he doing?" I asked.

His teacher folded her hands. "As you know, we like to have the kids engage with us on the smart board. When it comes to Josiah, I have to admit he doesn't engage with us nearly as much as we'd like.

"But something funny happened the other day. When someone came in to observe the class, we couldn't keep Josiah in his seat. He just kept jumping up out of turn. He'd zoom up quickly to the smart board and get the answer right every time.

"He loves when I read to him individually. That's when he engages me most. It's been fun to see his homework answers for the book *Hatchet*."

I gave her a weak smile. "I just wish he'd communicate with you like he does with me at home on the iPad."

The therapist became almost tearful. "Yeah, we really want to reach him. We know he's super smart, but we can't figure out the best way to connect. It doesn't help that he can be so uncooperative."

The room fell quiet. "Tell me more."

The therapist hesitated. "Well, I tell him to do one thing, and he often does the exact opposite."

"It's true," the teacher said, nodding. "Basically, the only times we get him to sit still for class activities is when he's sitting in the plastic storage tub. Otherwise, he'll dash off to the windowsill and jump like he's flying. As you can imagine, it disrupts the whole class."

"He gets into things," the therapist added. "We have to monitor our tissues and paper because he shoves them in his mouth. Also, we have to watch him in the bathroom because he sticks his hands in the toilet and splashes water all over."

The teacher offered a sympathetic look. "We have younger kindergarten-aged kids in the class. I think some of their noises and squeals set him off."

The therapist sighed. "Yeah, but we really need to do something about the hair pulling. Last week, he pulled an aide's hair so hard that she actually lost a chunk."

My shoulders tightened. *Oh God, please help me hold it together.*

"I'm sure he didn't mean anything by this," said his teacher reluctantly, "but the other day he even came down on my injured toe."

Well, that did it. My kettle was whistling now. Hot embarrassment crawled up my neck. How could my sweet son who loved Jesus and who had improved so much at home be the source of so much trouble in his classroom? Yes, I knew his behavior wasn't stellar—but this? It was totally unacceptable.

The teacher rested her hand on my shoulder. "I know this is hard to hear. We really don't want to be a downer, but we're running out of tricks."

I thanked them and cried all the way home.

Morning couldn't come fast enough to unleash my questions.

"Young man, we need to talk about what integrity means."

He didn't look away from his electric piano keys as he pounded them.

"Josiah, your teachers gave me a lot of bad reports, so I need to talk with you about what integrity means. Integrity is acting on the outside based on what you believe on the inside. It's when you're being the same person no matter who you're with. Can you tell me why you're showing more maturity at home but acting so out of line at school?"

He scooted close. **I am clarified in mind, but joyless in body. To say what you feel is to voice dear little blessings. It's hard to not express anything all day long, for I am not heard like this at school.**

**I am not mute in my mind, but that is the problem with autism. You get worked into hasty wailing because you can't speak in an instant. You want to throw a blaring tantrum so you can be heard like a real person.**

**Please help people understand this yearning that troubles the person with autism so much. It's not just being stirred up in thoughts only to voice failure with the body to perform. It is not just failure to speak. The orders to be totally still make you want to be even louder. It is the simple fear that muscle will be accepted over brain to speak of who I am.**

I nudged up his glasses. What exactly was I supposed to say to that? "I get it, JoJo. I really do. I know you wish things were set up differently at school, so you could communicate with them like you do with me. I know that's hard, but you still need to cooperate with them. We all know your body is uncooperative, but it sure doesn't sound like you're even trying your best right now."

**I'm sorry, Mom.**

"Do you hear me, Josiah? You need to always respect your earthly teachers, even if they aren't as perfect as your heavenly ones."

A groan escaped his throat.

**To be a good student is to voice daily work they would like to see. I am now voicing rich-ordered spelling, but I do understand that I need my work to be more like a fountain than a racetrack.**

**To voice fast feet all the time to my teachers is to be a racetrack. Loud is a racetrack. Fast is a racetrack. Crashing is a racetrack. Wild in the stands is a racetrack.**

**To help my teachers, I will try to do this real motion to be a fountain, not a racetrack, so I can try to voice my work.**

**I am sorry. Will you forgive me for my worrisome, troubled**

behaviors, teachers? I am sorry. Work is my worst main pride. I
am now so prideful to not let you teach me so I am trouble to you.

"It's good to hear you say you're sorry," I said. "But words are
cheap if actions don't follow. We need to start holding you more
accountable to what you say. Oh, and you need to try participating
in classwork and activities without being silly. I accept your apol-
ogy though. And I'll be sure to send it to your teachers."

Mom, blast this to Facebook. "Sorry" says a lot of things, but
the most important is that the tragic space between you and
God or you and others could never be so permanent that "sorry"
couldn't make a bridge.

When "sorry" is spoken, the bridge becomes a fast highway
for "hear" to courageously get to there.

Voicing it will make you a spunky, far-reaching teacher to
others who aren't sure how to voice it themselves.

In November, Joe and I gave ourselves a break and started
attending a couples Bible study. Not just any old study, but one
specifically for parents of kids with special needs.

In the past, just the two of us had studied an amazing book
about the battle in our minds. Because of our own issues, however,
we ironically always ended up in a fight afterward. This time was
different. We joined four other couples with special needs kids,
and we cracked open Ephesians to learn about allowing the Holy
Spirit to renew our thoughts and attitudes. More than anything, we
wanted to connect with people who understood our parental challenges, sleepless nights, marital strain, and desire to dream again.

We met at a local church where they provided a room for college volunteers to supervise all the kids. Josiah went willingly, and
we always knew we were just a few steps away if a problem arose.

One December night, after our DVD session, we went around
the table discussing our thoughts on growth and transformation.
One of the guys tearfully admitted he'd been struggling to trust God.

"As a husband and dad, you want to be able to fix things," he said. "I'm able to make things happen at my job because I can perform, but when it comes to my home job, I always feel like I'm failing. It's easy to get discouraged and impatient."

The other guys nodded, and I felt frustrated with the enemy for his unoriginal lies. These dads could do a thousand things right but at the same time experience the sinking belief that they couldn't solve the problem of their endless cycle of pain.

I loved so many things about this group, but I especially loved how God had led us here.

It happened in August when I drove to a park and Josiah refused to get out of the car. Too tired to push it, I drove to another park, but he still wouldn't get out.

I probably broke all the parenting rules, but I drove to a third park. This time, when I opened the door, Josiah sprung out with zest and raced to the playground like a completely different kid.

That's when I noticed a mom and dad with their special needs little girl. The mom had a kind face and the dad stood on the other side of the girl while the couple helped her onto the climber.

Josiah squealed, and I turned to see him attempt one of his high-flying routines on the jungle gym.

"Careful!" I hollered.

The mom looked at me with understanding while her daughter stared at Josiah, completely enamored.

"I'm Jamie," the mom said, extending her hand.

"Hi, I'm Tahni, and that live-wire dude up there is my son, Josiah."

She squinted her eyes, studying him. "Josiah? I know of a Josiah. He's from the Facebook page, *Josiah's Fire*. But it couldn't possibly be …"

"Yes!" I exclaimed. "That's my son's Facebook page."

She smiled. "No way. What are the odds? We've moved out of this neighborhood, so we hardly even come to this park."

"How did you hear about *Josiah's Fire*?"

"Well, our daughter has autism, so one of my workmates told me about it. I used to work in children's ministry."

"Wild," I said. "I used to work at a church too."

One conversation turned into several get-togethers. That's how she came to invite Joe and me to this new Bible study she and her husband started at her church.

Even now as I peered around the room, I felt utterly thankful at how God had led us to this place. I gave Joe a wink when it was his turn to speak.

"When it comes to growth, I feel like I've gone a bit backward," he admitted. "I used to be really into reading my Bible, memorizing Scripture, and nurturing my faith, but Josiah's autism diagnosis took a big toll on me. I ended up believing God had let me down—because that's what it felt like.

"Whenever we faced a need, Tahni would say, 'Let's pray,' and I'd say, 'Sure,' but to tell you the truth, I didn't believe anything would change. Sometimes we actually experienced the opposite of what we prayed for.

"Don't get me wrong, I'm thankful Josiah started communicating, but I'm still struggling with the fact that I don't feel the same bond with God that Josiah and Tahni have with him. That makes me feel left out and hurt sometimes. Because of that, I don't really try to grow closer to God. At least that's the way it's been."

After Joe and I settled in the car, I set my hand on his leg. "I'm really proud of you, Joe. You were super real and honest in sharing your feelings. You didn't try to say what you thought others wanted to hear. I so admire you for that."

The next morning while I was making lunches, Joe walked into the kitchen and gave me a peck on the cheek. "I think we should start praying together again."

I set down the peanut butter and called in Josiah. There, on the landing, the three of us huddled like ducks taking shelter from a storm.

"Father," Joe prayed. "Please bless us today. Josiah has been having a tough time at school. Help him know he's safe and 100 percent loved. Give him strength to listen to his teachers and behave like he should. Jesus, help us know you're right here with us. Oh, and please help the New York Giants to win this weekend. Amen."

Lucy barked, signaling the arrival of the school bus. I gave everybody a kiss and moved to the window to watch Joe lead Josiah to his regular seat at the front of the bus.

*God, that's a good man and a good dad right there. Would you please surprise him with an extra personal sense of your goodness?*

# 30

# Heaven Unsilenced

"Angels make tears into minutes of amens."
– Josiah Cullen

**Winter 2014**

"I think he's an indigo child." After I hung up the phone, Kim's words replayed in my mind. According to a video she'd recommended, Josiah fit the description: gifted, sensitive, intuitive, wise, spiritual, and mature beyond his years.

I didn't exactly see Josiah as an indigo child, but when I watched the film, it helped me better understand him and the things others believed.

Some psychologists believed these so-called indigo children had mental illnesses and anomalies, while others insisted that they experienced some kind of paranormal activity or evolution of consciousness. Frankly, words like *telepathic* and *clairvoyant* made me cringe. Were Josiah's experiences coming from God and his kingdom of light, or from some kind of "psychic" realm?

Before I had time to think much more about it, Josiah bounded in. I hadn't shared anything with him about Kim, so he knew nothing about our open conversations. As I waited for him to type, I thought about how much I appreciated Kim's professional insights and her heart to help us.

**Hi, Mom,** he typed. **Nope. Natural Kim is nice to ring you up to**

chat. My sullen millisecond mind mounts to say natural nope to my label of indigo. Loud nope.

Yes, Josiah is a brilliant mouthpiece of God. I am not an indigo. I am average boy named to a loud mission to make God real. Bearing his name, I will serve him all my life.

My loud bullies will know my name because they fear my mined-out life just might work like my king loudly wants it to work. Love would ring in the streets. Music would feel again. Lack would salivate for major newness of life. Moping would turn to joy.

My sameness will not be found on this earth. My saturated mind is daring him to fill it to overflow, but he fills it to my limits, not to my desires. You don't have to worry that my noggin will explode. He saves me to jaguar dare me to run to him now and always.

My God names no guru to be me. I am not a guru. I am not a vanishing medium. I am not a clairvoyant. I am not holier than my life's mounting-up tests.

Jesus calls me to the same holiness as any other person. My name is business-minded, music-minded, nationally-minded, church-minded, faith-minded, mega-breaker-of-autism-minded. My name is busy poet, musician of worship, seer, and daring boy that loves my God.

My name is Josiah. My mom is a pastor. My dad is a producer. My dog is a peacemaker.

Each day I am named as God's fire. Fire is carefully named to heat up, to destroy dead ground, to liven up radical change, to help make natural answers seem clear. Fire names gold as heated jewelry, silver as heated weapons, pottery as ware for portable goods.

No need to label me as indigo or heaven's valuable messenger, or thinking poet, or named boy prophet. I am just lit up by his fire. My life will need him in it all of my days.

Autism and ADD, natural men's labels, mean boy is dangerous

to his surroundings. My life is calculated to make my name synonymous with basic blessing.

My name is Josiah. My goal is to make him my raging Father by naming his gates to be fast, holy, and very open to all people who call him Father, call Jesus Son, and call Holy Spirit helper.

My basic name is this boy. I don't need a label to make this clearer. I am his fire, see. Are you naming me his fire? To say I am Josiah, which is God's fire, is to say my name and my goal.

"Josiah," I said, trying to process all this, "I know in the past you've talked about how you're like the fire of God. I'm wondering, did you know the meaning of your name? I thought you did."

God just told me this. I didn't know my name is God's fire, nor that my goal was contained in that name. Do you know Josiah means God's fire?

I nodded. "Yes, I sure do. We knew the meaning of it back when we gave you the name. Josiah means 'fire of the Lord.' I even used to sing it to you. 'Josiah, the fire of the Lord is upon you. The fire of the Lord is upon you now.'"

His mouth hung open as he typed. So you knew that? So I am named Josiah because you liked "fire of the Lord"? This is amazing, Mom. You needed to name me Josiah, and you didn't even know it. Real name, real call on my life, Mom.

Sameness is not King Josiah either. He was not like other kings. My namesake binged on God's laws, knew his name, saw his fire, and valued his holiness in all places of Jewish society. My namesake built my name up to me.

I remembered reading about the king's accomplishments while at Pacem in Terris. "JoJo, do you know anything else about King Josiah?"

I talked to him, Mom. He told me nominal kings not only make names for themselves, but they name their kingdoms to be their buildings, their barns, their temples to many gods, their business, their busts to legend, making them immortalized.

Basically, King Josiah told me times vanished when business

became God, when daily vagueness became faith, when basic religion became artful national theological meanness.

My job was his job. Naming me Josiah was a great seeing into my directives. Entire salute to that choice.

"Thanks," I said, straightening his shirt. "And your daddy and I salute how well you carry out the meaning of your name."

God gave me salivating moments in his presence to say he is a consuming fire. My God is a javelin between acts and faith.

He is the reason vultures might prey on me, but it makes no difference. He is not making boy march to any drum, so no handsome javelin that tries to name me anything can claim my Jesus-named faith. I have no market I belong to. I am God's fire, and he can't name fire if it is not all consuming.

God says no man can live and not see brightness of God's majesty at least once before they die. Man makes no mistake or no large "Dang, I missed him." They see his glory, Mom, at least once in their lives.

They will need him or they will make it majorly loud that they don't. His life in them is big if they need him. It is small if they kind of need him. It is nothing if they need him in no way.

Men never die nimbly making no thought to his existence. It is impossible. He is not marginal to men, not now, not then, not ever.

What a big name God gave me, Mom. God's fire.

That night as I lay in bed listening to the wind rattle my window, Josiah's words danced in my head like blazing flames, calling me to wonder what I'd wondered a thousand times: How could Josiah keep experiencing heaven in such a profound way and not be healed?

My iPad glowed under the sheets like the full moon I'd seen at Sue Rampi's a few nights back. After I had said goodbye to the ladies, I stood in her driveway, gazing at the textured orb of light, thanking God for its beauty and for each opportunity he gave me to speak into the lives of others.

Something strange happened the next morning. Josiah, who hadn't known about my ponderings in Sue's driveway, woke up and wrote about how he had seen me gazing at the moon talking to Jesus.

"H-how did you know this?" My words tumbled out in breathless awe. "How did you see it?" I watched as the answer trickled out.

**From heaven. Yes, directly when you looked up. Jesus let me see you. Minister of gospel attended by ladies was being ministered to as well by the beautiful moon.**

Beneath the sheets in the stillness of night, I scrolled through Josiah's past entries, and felt jarred by one of his reflections.

**Hours at school are bright but not happy to my soul. Break my heart, my great big nice school needs my great big nice self to be nice, but my niceness gets no one to listen to me.**

**Lift me up sometimes, will you? I need a hug. My nights are bigly much much louder than my days.**

I pressed my eyes closed. *Oh, Father. My son has such a hard time at school. It's hard enough for someone like him to handle his uncooperative body, but how in the world is someone who regularly experiences heaven supposed to deal with all of his limitations? I beg you again, please heal him.*

From the deepest pit of my pain, I thought of David composing his psalms. How could he have gone from feeling God didn't care about him to confidently asserting that the world's Creator was intimately involved in every detail of his life?

My old art gallery dream popped back in my mind. Perhaps King David personally understood that God doesn't create in straight lines. As for me, well, I was starting to.

*Father, in the midst of this long-pressing night, I choose to worship you, no matter how messy I find the lines of my life. You are great. You are mighty. Your life-giving voice is powerful and majestic. When I consider the heavens, what is man that you are mindful of him? Oh, how you care for us.*

The following morning, I changed Josiah's overnight diaper and followed him to our couch, which had become so worn out you could see his butt imprint.

He propped an elbow on my knee. Even after all this time, I still had to support his arm. More than ever, I felt God's support on my own life. The Lord, the Word made flesh, had been teaching me to freefall into his safety net of grace.

Josiah let out a long low groan as he typed.

**Mom, talk to me. Class told me my work needs to be made into music now, like real music. For the mute mouth will make a joyful noise for my God. Lend an ear. That mute is me.**

**Fundamentally, I am not mute in spirit, so I am not mute to God. Not at all. So why do I muster up so much stirring for my words to come? Sweet words shall come, truly they will, but my voice is already in my spirit. It is beautiful. It is loud. It is yet to be found by the world, but God hears it.**

**Wrestling for the mute mouth is like wrestling for the name that says, "Poor child." I am not poor, so I am not mute really. So I am now to be mostly singing for joy to be made full by my simple, daily worship so I can tell my words.**

"Oh, Josiah," I said. "My wrestling worshiper, you grip my soul." I gave him a tight hug and finally let go, so he could continue.

**You love the child you have, so you will have the child you love. It is what God does for us. He loves the me I am, so I can be the me he sees I am.**

**Though I am not so mute inside, to be so voted is to become a daring project. So the project becomes the focus when the person is to be the focus.**

**In the fullness of man is the glory of his maker, for he is not small at all. He is large. Man is small, but man is made to be so much more than these senses tell him to be. So is the future of this earth to understand that you and I are not under Satan's mutiny. We are the future found in God's majesty, and in it I am set free.**

**Hold my hand. Like it or not, I am broken, but he is true. I am to be so whole in that reality, so I will be. For I am now the fullness of God in Christ to say that while dangerous times ordered my worst nudges to be quiet inside my world, I broke out to say, "I am that boy that sounds the loud trumpet. Words are not you. They are him to your world. You are him to your world when you speak like him." That is all there is to it. Heaven is now unsilenced.**

My hand trembled as it slid over his, absorbing his warmth. I had nothing to say except a silent *Thank you, Jesus*. None of us knew when Josiah's full healing would come. We simply knew it would.

Just like we knew, with all of heaven behind us, God had only great things in mind—and with our hands secured tightly in his, we could lift our heads and fully trust his ever-reaching love.

"Great big love breaks Hiroshima bombs to bits.
Mighty love, like fire, gets hot when it gets oxygen.
Jesus blows the breath of God on thinking about love."
– Josiah Cullen

# DISCUSSION GUIDE

1. During her storm Tahni felt distanced from God. How did he come through for her? Read Psalm 30. In what ways has God come through for you in your hardships?

2. How did having a child with a disability impact Tahni's relationships? How have trials impacted yours?

3. Read Proverbs 31:8–9. Josiah's inability to speak often left him feeling misunderstood. In what ways can you speak up for those who don't have a voice?

4. Describe Tahni's quest to hear God's voice. John 10:1–16 tells us we can hear God's voice and how certain voices are best ignored. How do you mostly hear from God, and how has this changed over time?

5. Describe Tahni's quest for Josiah's healing in comparison to your beliefs and experiences. In what ways can you keep faith alive while you wait for God to answer your prayers? Discuss Luke 18:1–8.

6. *Josiah's Fire* is filled with the supernatural. Which of the Cullens' experiences affected you most and why? How did the book stretch or influence your views?

7. Josiah has a prophetic gift. In what ways is this shown in the book? What does the New Testament say about prophecy? (Read John 11:51; Acts 2:17–18; Romans 12:6; 1 Corinthians 12:4–11; 1 Corinthians 14:5, 29–33; 2 Peter 1:19–21.) Have you known anybody with this gift?

8.  1 Corinthians 13:2 shows that prophecy must always
    be demonstrated out of love. How did Josiah model
    this? How did *Josiah's Fire* encourage you to think or act
    differently about prophecy?

9.  God showed Tahni through Josiah that she is a princess.
    Name some ways in which God has intervened to show
    you your true value.

10. Josiah's first sentence "God is a good gift giver" reminds us
    of James 1:17: "Every good and perfect gift is from above,
    coming down from the Father of the heavenly lights, who
    does not change like the shifting shadows." How does
    living in the knowledge of God's goodness affect your daily
    life?

11. God repeatedly surprises us in ways the world might
    consider foolish (1 Corinthians 1:27). For example, God
    tells us we must become like little children to enter the
    kingdom of heaven (Matthew 18:3). What does this
    peculiar verse mean to you?

12. Hebrews 1:14 describes angels as "ministering spirits
    sent to serve those who will inherit salvation." How did
    Tahni react when Josiah saw angels? How do you think
    you would react? How does having an awareness of angels
    affect your life?

13. Hebrews 12:1 tells us we're surrounded by a great
    cloud of witnesses, heroes of the faith who have passed
    on. According to the second part of this verse, how is
    this awareness supposed to help us? Which of Josiah's
    explanations or descriptions about loved ones in heaven
    stuck with you most? Do you think Hebrews 12:1 could
    apply to your loved ones?

14. What are some of your favorite Scriptures about heaven? Which of Josiah's words or poems about heaven meant the most to you, and why?

15. Who is the first person you'd like to talk to in heaven? What is one pressing question you'd like to ask?

16. What did Josiah tell Tahni he saw in her mansion? If heaven contains some of the favorite things we loved on earth, what might you expect to find there?

17. Of all the chapters in *Josiah's Fire*, which one affected you most, and why?

18. How could you creatively use this book to brighten someone's day or influence him/her for eternity?

# FROM THE AUTHORS

God wasn't kidding when he told the prophet Isaiah, "As the heavens are higher than the earth, so are my ways higher than your ways and my thoughts than your thoughts."

I thought I might one day self-publish our story to preserve Josiah's words and the powerful things God was doing in our family, but the idea of coauthoring the full jaw-dropping account with all its wild twists and turns never crossed my mind. That is, until I spoke at a Christian Women in Media event and met writer Cheryl Ricker.

Working with Cheryl has been an amazing dream partnership that turned into a lasting genuine friendship. We diligently and continuously sought God's guidance for this book, wanting nothing less than his perfect plan.

Despite Cheryl's ever-present voice recorder, she always made me feel at ease during the interviews. She didn't furrow her brow or try to debate our experience. Instead she listened and even affirmed it, showing she could handle the "far-out" risky nature of writing this kind of a true-life story.

Committed to truth, Cheryl displayed a master ability to ask key questions, craft the right words, write the most compelling story that captures my voice, and always stay true to Josiah's writings as well.

My heart overflows with thanks to Cheryl and both of our husbands, Joe and Dwight, who tirelessly linked arms with us on this venture.

Josiah's words have become forever knit to my heart; and Cheryl's words are knit to us too, making this book a three-strand cord from the Lord that will now strengthen many.

– Tahni Cullen

When God said, "Cheryl, I have something exciting for you at this Christian Women in Media event," he wasn't kidding either.

Tahni might have been a surprise fill-in for a speaker with a family emergency, but nothing was an accident. I instantly fell in love with Tahni's honesty, compassion, and Jesus-zest. Two weeks later, as I interviewed her in my home, I sensed a match made in heaven and knew God would lead us.

After I transcribed the interviews and prayerfully planned each chapter, Tahni went in for more rounds of my hard-hitting questions, often answering in written form so I could maximize details and unpack extra layers for my novel-like style.

Meanwhile her fire-hose son, Josiah, kept typing a steady stream of rock-your-world prophetic messages, giving trooper Tahni the arduous task of deciphering them, adding spaces, punctuation, and paragraphs before sending them to me so I could ask God to highlight what he wanted to include in *Josiah's Fire*.

What a unique opportunity to see parts of the story unfold before my eyes. The more it did, the more I saw Josiah's words as a gift that could transform even the most hopeless hearts.

When Josiah instructed me to look for a publisher with the most joy and enthusiasm about a little boy going to heaven, BroadStreet rose miles above the competition. From day one, our BroadStreet family cherished this gripping story and us, its simple carriers.

We pray its unforgettable truth spills powerful comfort, peace, and joy into your life—directly from the heart of our loving, limitless Lord.

– Cheryl Ricker

# ABOUT THE AUTHORS

**Tahni Cullen** is a people-lover, blogger, and conference speaker who brings a powerful message of hope and restoration. Tahni worked for thirteen years at a multi-campus church in the Twin Cities of Minnesota, serving in communication arts and as a ministry director. She is a freelance marketer and also performs in an original live variety show for women's events. Tahni and her producer husband, Joe, have created an award-winning documentary called *Surprised by Autism*. They live with their son, Josiah, in Saint Paul, where they enjoy exploring Minnesota's museums and destinations.

**Cheryl Ricker** is an author, blogger, speaker, and poet who enjoys all things artsy. She writes supernatural true-life stories that ignite people's passion to pursue God. Her first book of this genre, *Rush of Heaven: One Woman's Miraculous Encounter with Jesus*, reveals that with God, all things are possible. Cheryl studied creative writing at York University in Toronto, Ontario, and theology at Christ for the Nations Institute in Dallas, Texas. When Cheryl is not writing books, painting with watercolors, or sharing her faith, she loves having heart-to-heart conversations with her husband and two sons at their home in southeast Minnesota.

JosiahsFire.com